CW00337884

If it is profit that a man is after, he should become a merchant, and if he does the job of a bookseller then he should renounce the name of poet. Christ forbid that the business followed by such creatures should furnish a man of spirit with his occupation.

Every year I spend a fortune, and so it would be a fine thing if I followed the example of the gambler who placed a bet of a hundred ducats and then beat his wife for not filling the lamps with the cheapest oil.

So print my letters carefully, on good parchment, and that's the only recompense I want. In this way bit by bit you will be the heir to all my talent may produce.

ARETINO
from a letter dated 22nd June 1537, sent from Venice

LETTERS FROM THE PALAZZO BARBARO

Henry James

LETTERS FROM THE PALAZZO BARBARO

Edited by Rosella Mamoli Zorzi

Pushkin Press

London

© Copyright Alexander R. James,
Leon Edel and the Belknap Press of Harvard University Press
Foreword © Copyright 1989, Leon Edel
Introduction © Copyright 1998, Rosella Mamoli Zorzi

First published in 1998 by
Pushkin Press
71-75 Shelton Street
London WC2H 9JQ

This edition published in 2012

British Library Cataloguing in Publication Data: A catalogue record
for this book is available from the British Library

ISBN 978 1 908968 89 0

All rights reserved. No part of this publication may be
reproduced, stored in a retrieval system or transmitted in
any form or by any means, electronic, mechanical,
photocopying, recording or otherwise,
without prior permission in writing from
Pushkin Press

Frontispiece: *Henry James* (1913) by John Singer Sargent
© National Portrait Gallery, London
Photographs © Osvaldo Böhm Agency, Venice and Patricia Curtis

Set in 10.5 on 13.5 Monotype Baskerville by M Rules
Proudly printed and bound in Great Britain by TJ International,
Padstow, Cornwall on Munken Premium White 90gsm

www.pushkinpress.com

ACKNOWLEDGEMENTS

I would like to dedicate the English, revised version of this book to the memory of Leon Edel, without whose encouragement I would never have proceeded along the path of Jamesian studies. And my gratitude to Alexander R. James, who has generously given his permission for the publication of James's work for this book, and on previous occasions.

I would like to thank the Directors of the following Institutions for their permissions to publish these letters, for the joy of working in their libraries, and their staff for their helpfulness: the Houghton Library of Harvard University, the Dartmouth College Library, the C. W. Barrett Library of the University of Virginia, the Isabella Stewart Gardner Museum, the Ashmolean Museum of Oxford, and the *Biblioteca Nazionale Marciana* in Venice.

Finally, my gratitude for initiating my Jamesian interests goes to Sergio Perosa (Ca' Foscari University), and to Alide Cagidemetrio (University of Udine) and Werner Sollors (Harvard University) for their intelligent and affectionate help and advice.

Patricia Curtis Viganò and Carlo Viganò—and the wide-open marble arms of their Palazzo Barbaro—were a constant source of encouragement for which I am truly thankful.

I would also like to thank Marina Coslovi for her help in preparing the text.

Rosella Mamoli Zorzi
June 1998

CONTENTS

Foreword by Leon Edel   13

Introduction by Rosella Mamoli Zorzi   19

Letters by Henry James   57

Letters by the Curtises   171

Notes by Ariana Curtis   205

Notes by Patricia Curtis Viganò   213

Index   218

Façade, Palazzo Barbaro

FOREWORD

BY LEON EDEL

This book celebrates a single palace in Venice—the Palazzo Barbaro, whose steps are washed by the Grand Canal. A modest, thick-walled palace with two striking rows of Gothic windows, it was built in the fifteenth century and survived the turbulent years of the wars with the Turks and the fatal Venetian conquest of Lombardy. In the quietude of Venice's decline, it became—in the 1880s—the residence of American expatriates, children of a new empire of commerce. Perhaps Venice seemed to them to have some of the uniqueness they imparted to Boston, for the Barbaro might have been called in the late nineteenth century an outpost of Boston. It was purchased by two proper Bostonians, Daniel Curtis and his wife Ariana and at times they rented it to another Bostonian, the bejewelled and queenly Isabella Stewart Gardner, who in the end would build her own Venetian palace, Fenway Court, in her home city.

An entire book might be written about the relations between Venice and its Americans, but Rosella Mamoli Zorzi has chosen to offer us a modest gathering-in of certain letters written by members of the trans-Atlantic society who were joined by certain British figures in the high-ceilinged drawing room of the Barbaro's *piano nobile*. Here Robert Browning, friend of another American expatriate in Venice, Mrs Bronson, came for tea and chatted about commonplace things; here John Addington Symonds, the historian of the Italian renaissance, a Victorian with a "secret life" and his friend Horatio Brown, frequently dined. And here Henry James, the American novelist of international *moeurs*, sometimes came for long visits. A compulsive letter-writer, he is at the very centre of Rosella Zorzi's anthology, for he provides vivid documentation of that particular society.

James came to Venice at first simply as a tourist. Returning in the 1880s he took possession of the city as he had of the Old World and in this instance in language uncommonly erotic for a man of his reticence—"you desire to embrace it, to caress it, to possess it." From that time on Venice became one of his regular way-stations on the Continent. At one moment he even dreamed of finding a *pied-à-terre* such as he gave to his character Merton Densher near the Rialto. However he found something better. The Palazzo Barbaro and its high life-style was always open to him. The Curtises liked his elegance, and his grand way of saying things. He, in turn, fell in with the idiosyncrasies of Daniel Curtis, with his twice-told anecdotes, his exploits as a gardener in a city that has little land for gardening, and his irascible criticisms of their mutual United States. James in particular liked the Barbaro itself—its cool high rooms, the cushioned seats inside the Gothic windows and the balcony from which he watched the traffic of the Grand Canal and the doings of neighbours in the shabby row of palaces across the way. He had feelings of grandeur, princely feelings, as he mounted the massive staircase in the Barbaro's inner courtyard. That allowed him direct access to the *piano nobile*.

He also stayed at the Barbaro when Isabella Gardner held court in it during her summer rentals. Life in the Barbaro was American at its most sophisticated, even if touched by certain provincialisms. But then, Venice itself, shorn of *imperium*, seemed a provincial city, an adorable place outside and beyond the rest of the world. For James, the Piazza San Marco was "the drawing-room of Europe" and he tells us that the great square with its wheeling and floating pigeons had witnessed "more of the joy of life than in any equal area in Europe." We pause over this, for territorially the Square would be less than a pinhead on the map of Europe. Nevertheless the joy he spoke of must have been intense, at least for *him*—and it certainly was visible in the faces of tourists who filled the piazza every day and night.

This was the public life of Venice. Novelists like James, however, are always in search of private lives, or as he put it "we peep at most into two or three of the chambers of their hospitality." Still, he could endow his heroine in *The Wings of the Dove* with his own examination of the ceiling in the Barbaro library where on one occasion Isabella put in a bed for him, all the other guest rooms being occupied. We know he greatly enjoyed this experience for he dwells in his novel on the arabesques, medallions and the play of light "on the stirred sea-water, flickering up through open windows" and relishes "the nest of white cherubs set in their great moulded and figured concavity." In one letter to Isabella he remembers the pink chairs and the yellow sofa and a glimpse of her queenly self in a gauze dressing gown on a blue chair.

We are committed to verbal pictures. We remind ourselves however that John Singer Sargent was a friend of the Curtises and he painted them under the great chandeliers in the drawing-room, Daniel and Ariana, and their son Ralph and his wife, a fine painting, highly documentary, of 1899. Another painter, during one of Isabella's sojourns, Anders Zorn, from Sweden, has left us a portrait of the lady floating in through the curtains of one of the windows.

Such is the testimony of brush and pen to what James

called "the poetry of the thing outlived and lost and gone." He finished *The Aspern Papers* in the Barbaro in 1887; and during another visit wrote *A London Life* at an oriental desk probably plundered centuries before in the east.

This volume now becomes a part of our testimony. However we cannot recover the talk or the nights when hundreds of candles were lit and the music of hired musicians or visiting celebrities could be heard as it floated through the delicately-shaped windows over the water. Royalty too came to the Barbaro: we can instance, among visits from the north, Queen Victoria's daughter, the one who briefly was Empress of Germany, adorning the drawing-room, surrounded by awe and honor. But there is in this volume also a "peep" at Henry James himself through the eyes of the young Ralph Curtis. In one of his letters he describes the novelist as haunted by "the printer's devil." And then he adds "what a pity he knew no other." It is an observation for biographers and their meditations. Rosella Zorzi's anthology sets us dreaming of the beautiful preserved city, its Grand Canal, the bridges and footways, and the ghosts that now exist only in old documents as Venice, on its treacherous sea, is translated into enduring literature.

Early twentieth century view of the Palazzo Barbaro

INTRODUCTION

BY ROSELLA MAMOLI ZORZI

There is a palazzo, on the Grand Canal, quite close to the Accademia Bridge, which looks over the vast ribbon of the Grand Canal where it widens into the Bacino of St. Mark's. If you lean out just a little from the balcony of its Gothic windows, you will see the magnificent structure of the Salute church across the water, near the Punta della Dogana. Then your eyes, coming back along the Canal, will take in the façades of the Gothic Palazzo Semitecolo, the Wolkoff, the multicoloured and now infamous Dario, the unfinished majesty of the Venier dei Leoni (now the Peggy Guggenheim Museum), the modest Casa Biondetti— once the home of painter Rosalba Carriera—the imposing Gothic façade of Palazzo Da Mula, and then, beyond the Canal of San Vio, the façades of Ca' Loredan and Contarini dal Zaffo, stopping in front of the Accademia bridge.

Your gaze, turning into the interior of the palace after being dazzled by the view outside of the Grand Canal, will not find a rest: the glimmering splendour of the water and the bright colours of the marble façades are replicated in the glory of the gilded *stuccoes*, of the paintings, of the mother-of-pearl floors. The dazzle will only relent in the slightly damp penumbra of the courtyard, when you descend the steep, open staircase, or in the shadowy light which filters through the long ground-floor passageway leading to the palazzo's water gate. In that passageway a grounded gondola, with its black *felze* still there to protect its passengers from wind and rain, seems to be waiting for a Domenico or an Angelo to row it back into its natural element, the water of the Grand Canal.

This palace, Palazzo Barbaro, is only one of the many patrician houses that testify to the former greatness of Venetian families and of a civilization tracing back many generations. It is also one of the many palaces that were sold after the fall of the Venetian Republic in 1797 and which fell into the greedy hands of speculators, who did not hesitate to sell off and disperse the memories of centuries of history, the family archives, paintings, art objects, antique furniture. The very walls of these palaces were plundered: the *stucco* work was chiselled off, the frescoes were torn down, the inlaid wooden doors were lifted off their iron hinges; whole buildings were razed and the bricks and stones were used as building materials.

Until 1797 the Palazzo Barbaro had witnessed centuries of splendour. In the fifteenth century it had been the meeting point for some of the most illustrious representatives of Renaissance humanism. These scholars had been drawn to the house by the bright mind of Almorò Barbaro, who meditated on the chapters of Aristotle which he would expound, in the original Greek, to his disciples from the University of Padua while walking to and fro in his grand salon. To this house came Poliziano[1], to receive a Greek vase from the hands of Almorò's father, Zaccaria, the Procuratore of San Marco, an illustrious politician and the son of the first Venetian humanist, Francesco. Zaccaria was the Barbaro who, around 1460, had originally bought the palace that would carry his family's name for so many centuries.

From that date the salons of the palace echoed with debates regarding the noblest themes of culture and the most important political issues.

In the 1540s, in these rooms, Daniele, the ambassador of the Venetian Republic to England, later the Patriarch Elect of Aquileia, gathered the founders of modern mathematics and architecture. A friend and a patron of Palladio and Scamozzi, Daniele obtained for them the great public commissions of Venice. His own translation of, and commentary on, Vitruvius's *Treaty on Architecture* was extremely influential. In the same period, his brother Marc'Antonio devoted himself to diplomacy and politics, becoming a Procuratore of

San Marco. Splendid and cultured, he shared and supported his brother's choices, and with him he decided to build the famous Villa of Maser, designed by Palladio, with frescoes by Veronese. Half a century later, another Barbaro, Antonio, an opponent of the great general Francesco Morosini, had the baroque church of Santa Maria del Giglio built to celebrate the family.

Voices full of wisdom, knowledge, and power resounded within the damask-lined walls of the palace, against its Istria stone balconies, on its terrazzo floors. The century of baroque splendour brought sumptuous embellishments to the house, clear signs of the great power of the family. At the end of the seventeenth century, the architect Antonio Gaspari was commissioned to build the great ballroom, linking two adjacent palaces. Artists in *stucco* work from Ticino were called to decorate the ballroom walls with shells and putti and ribbons and gilded triumphs—just as in the Albrizzi and Sagredo palaces or at the Scuola dei Carmini— while great masters were entrusted with the paintings and frescoes. Giambattista Tiepolo, Gian Battista Piazzetta, Sebastiano Ricci and Antonio Balestra were among them. The perfect taste of the Barbaros chose the best artists of each generation.[2]

Then, after all this glory of culture, politics, and art, ruin descended on the palazzo. After 1861, the palace was sold several times, into the clutches of unscrupulous antique dealers. Among these some tried to tear down the *stucco* work to sell it to the London South Kensington Museum (now the Victoria & Albert Museum), but the palace did not allow them to do this: it was simply impossible to detach the *stucco* work. The greed of one dealer saved the great doors: he thought the 17,000 lire offered by Lady Alford too low a price.[3] But the Tiepolos were sold, the courtyard well-head removed, hoisted onto a big black boat, and taken away; the ceiling was partly covered with bitumen, because the people who had moved into the palace did not like being "spied" upon by the allegorical figures flying above them in the painted skies[4].

The ruin of the palace seemed unavoidable. On a December afternoon in 1885, "buyers and sellers, lawyers and witnesses" met to draw up a sale contract. Palazzo Barbaro, then the property of "Cav. Dott. Cesare Musatti" through his wife, was sold to an American couple, Daniel Sargent Curtis and Ariana Wormeley Curtis.

The palace was saved.

If Daniel and Ariana were certain they had made a good investment, for the palace it was the height of good fortune to end up in the hands of a couple who loved it, restored it, and respected it. They were determined not to redo it completely as was the custom with those nineteenth-century owners and architects against whom Ruskin had fought his battles, together with Alvise Piero Zorzi in Venice.[5] The Curtises transformed the palace again and made it into a centre of elegant social life, but they also invited artists, writers, poets, painters, and musicians. These artists caught and expressed the essence of the Barbaro, in paintings and novels, building the Barbaro of their imagination, of pigments and words.

The Barbaro salons with their frescoes and paintings and *stucco* work fascinated such painters as John Singer Sargent, who portrayed the Curtises, with their son Ralph, a painter himself, and his wife Lisa, in the splendour of the ballroom, in the painting entitled *An Interior in Venice* (1899). The palace also enchanted Anders Zorn, who portrayed Isabella Stewart Gardner, the creator of Fenway Court at Boston and who occasionally rented the palace, as she stepped in from the palazzo balcony, against the nocturnal background of the Grand Canal lit up by fireworks. Other painters, such as Walter Gay, or Ralph Latimer, offered other interpretations: Gay painted the ballroom, with its paintings, *stucco* work, sofas, chairs and tables, without any human figure in it, as if the beauty of the place was enough. Latimer, Ralph Curtis's cousin, painted several rooms of the Barbaro.[6]

JAMES'S ARRIVAL IN VENICE

But the artist who more than anyone else filtered through his imagination the enchantment of the "marble halls" of the Barbaro was the American writer, Henry James (1843–1916). After a first visit in 1887 he was often a guest of the Curtises or of Isabella Stewart Gardner.

The impressions that James had of the Barbaro— over a period of several years—can be traced in his letters, which, although they are not entirely devoted to this topic, bear witness to the power of the Barbaro over the writer's imagination.

In James's letters[7] to Catherine Walsh (VII), Grace Norton (IX), and Ariana Curtis (XIV, XV) "the beautiful empty Barbaro", "all marbles and frescoes and portraits of the Doges", starts to exercise a charm that "sinks into your spirit only as you go on living there, seeing it in all its hours and phases" (III, 195). These words appear, almost identical, in his essay *The Grand Canal* (1892),—where the name of the palace is not given, out of respect for the Curtises' privacy— but where the Barbaro is clearly recognizable with its "painted chambers that still echo with one of the historic names":

"As you live in it day after day its beauty and its interest sink more deeply into your spirit; it has its moods and its hours and its mystic voices and its shifting expressions . . .
"If in the absence of its masters you have happened to have it to yourself for twenty-four hours you will never forget the charm of its haunted stillness, late on the summer afternoon for instance, when the call of playing children comes in behind from the campo, nor the way the old ghosts seemed to pass on tiptoe on the marble floors."[8]

In the summer of 1892 Isabella Stewart Gardner, having the house chock-full of guests, had a canopied bed, with a pink mosquito net[9], placed in "the divine old library", on the top floor, a room also decorated with delicate *stucco* medallions and eighteenth century *boiseries à la chinoise*. James spent delightfully quiet days there, in spite of the scorching scirocco, allowing the beauty of the place to sink into himself, almost passively. He wrote about it, with some humour, to Mrs. Curtis (XV), telling her that she, the real mistress of the house, did not know her own house at all:

"Have you ever *lived* here?—if you haven't, if you haven't gazed upward from your couch, in the rosy dawn, or during the postprandial (that is after luncheon) siesta, at the medallions and arabesques of the ceiling, permit me to tell you that you don't *know* the Barbaro."

The enchantment Palazzo Barbaro exercised on the writer is parallel with that wrought on him by the whole city: James started to dream about having his own *pied-à-l'eau* in Venice (XIII, XIV, XVII, XIX).

The young James arriving in 1869 in Italy, and in Venice for the first time aged twenty-five, found that Venice was "quite the Venice of one's dreams", although it remained "strangely the Venice of dreams, more than of any appreciable reality".[10] At that time he felt the need to declare to his brother the sense of his "yankeehood", which did not allow him to enjoy Venice from the inside, as a part of his own civilization, unlike his experience in England (Letter I). This statement was at least partly contradicted by the ecstatic tone with which James wrote to his brother, in the very same letter, of the deep and overwhelming impression made on him by Tintoretto. The enormous mass of Tintoretto's works was looked at by James in the wake of Ruskin.[11] It was not a coincidence that

James adored Tintoretto as a colourist and also for his extraordinary perspectives, or points of view, and the compositions of his paintings:[12] in his enthusiasm for Tintoretto, James seemed to see the extraordinary achievements in the use of viewpoint that would characterize the twentieth century novel, which owed so much to James himself.

No doubt James was *conquered* by, or gave himself up to Venice gradually, contrary to his response to Rome, as expressed in his famous and oft-quoted letter, where he declared "At last—for the first time—I live!"[13]

By the 1890s, James had had the opportunity of enjoying the city during various visits, staying in different houses: he no longer used the lodgings of Casa Barbesi, or the rooms on the Riva degli Schiavoni where he had been vainly trying to write *The Portrait of a Lady*. He had enjoyed the hospitality of Mrs. Bronson's Casa Alvisi, on the Grand Canal, right across from the Salute, and then that of the Curtises at Palazzo Barbaro. He had had the time to possess himself of the city, writing on it on several occasions, in the essays, from *Venice: an Early Impression* in 1872 to *Venice* in 1882 and *The Grand Canal* in 1892, where the writer took his reader along the main watery thoroughfare of Venice as if he were following one of those nineteenth century guides illustrating the main palaces on both sides of the Canal, from its beginning, at San Marco, to the Accademia and Rialto and finally to the Station. By 1892 James had written both short stories and novels at least partly set in Venice, and above all *The Aspern Papers* (1888). Perhaps towards the end of the 1880s or at the beginning of the 1890s James really dreamed of having a small *pied-à-terre* in Venice. But in the summer of 1893 he acknowledged this wish was a mere dream, "fading a little" (XIX) when he was not there.

Other, tragic, experiences intervened to defeat the dream. On January 24th, 1894, Constance Fenimore Woolson, an American writer, a descendant of James Fenimore Cooper, and a dear friend of James, committed suicide, throwing herself out of the window of Palazzo Semitecolo.[14] James had in 1886 shared a house with her, Villa Brichieri, at Bellosguardo, living however on different floors. James's letters to Mrs. Bronson (XXI, XXII) do not hide or mask the impression of horror which Miss Woolson's death had wrought on James. A sense of horror clearly accompanied by a sense of guilt—it does not matter whether justified or not—that crops up also in the long explanation of Miss Woolson's death that James felt himself impelled to give to Mrs. Bronson a few days after her suicide. The act, according to James, was caused by "some violent cerebral derangement", and everything seemed to prove this since Miss Woolson, a successful writer, was "*liked*, peculiarly, by people who knew her", and her relations "adored her". James seems to wish to persuade Mrs. Bronson, but above all himself, that a person so beloved by everybody should not have expected any love from *himself.* The "strange obscurity" of the facts covers up the difficulty of a relationship that seems to have become clear to James only after Miss Woolson's death, with the sudden violence, which the reader will find in such a story as *The Beast in the Jungle.*

Miss Woolson's death marked, for James, a period of detachment from Venice, or even of horror towards it. On July 29, 1894, James wrote to Mrs. Gardner (**XXIII**). Not only will he not be in Venice when "Mrs. Jack" holds her court at Palazzo Barbaro, but perhaps he will not return, ever, to Venice, because the city has been "simply blighted": a beautiful flower, killed by the frost of death. To Mrs. Curtis, James wrote: "How strange and empty Venice seemed to me, without you. The light is white and absent . . .".[15] The "bright Venetian air" has lost its splendour and colour. Even Palazzo Barbaro is "lovelier than ever— but what's the use?" What James did not write to Mrs. Gardner in his letter was what he had been doing in the three months he had spent in Venice, staying in that Casa Biondetti where Miss Woolson had lived before moving to Palazzo Semitecolo, and where he had acted as her literary executor. More than one contemporary witness wrote of James recounting in a suppressed, devious way, of the "execution", or suppression of, Miss Woolson's papers—and even of her black clothes[16]—in the black waters of the lagoon. One can add Zina Hulton's version:

"Then he [Henry James] told me that when he had sorted out a few manuscripts of hers [Miss Woolson's] which were complete, there remained a great mass of notes and commencements and other worthless fragments. After thinking the question over, he decided to destroy all these by drowning them in the lagoon. So he went far out in a gondola and committed them to the water where it was really deep."[17]

Death, the cancellation of what is dearest to a writer, his or her work, is represented by drowning in the deepest waters of the lagoon. The story of James's relationship with Venice becomes gloomy, ominous. Gone is the "bright Venetian air".

PALAZZO BARBARO AND
THE WINGS OF THE DOVE

James's relationship with Venice revived only after a period of time. The enchantment of Palazzo Barbaro merged with the experience of Miss Woolson's death. Miss Woolson's death recalled other deaths, such as that of Minnie Temple, James's cousin, in his youth,[18] and other impressions and emotions, to produce a masterpiece. James's great narrative art drew on these different experiences, at the time when the writer was the absolute master of form[19] and language, to produce *The Wings of the Dove*, the supreme homage to Venice and to Palazzo Barbaro: the supreme homage, because in this novel James built a palazzo made of words which is more real and enduring than that made of bricks and Istria stone and gilded *stucchi*.

James gives the name "Palazzo Leporelli" to the historic Venetian dwelling of the novel where Milly Theale, the young heiress who knows she has little time left, decides to live as much as she can and to live out her final days. The palace is the "great gilded shell" where Milly "with servants, frescoes, tapestries, antiquities, the thorough make-believe of a settlement", locks herself in, almost as if "in a fortress", in the "ark of her deluge", a place where she can "float on and on", with the feeling that has become a metaphor, of "never going down, of remaining aloft in the divine, dustless air, where she would hear but the splash of the water against stone".[20]

Palazzo Leporelli, the quintessence of the "dream city", as James had written to La Farge in 1869, is Milly's extreme effort to resist death and at the same time to taste life. She is "the priestess" who sees the work of art as the centre of her ritual. Palazzo Leporelli is an "appearance" which is not only the city's ambiguous reflection of herself in the water, but also that of life and above all of art.

James's long description of the palace is written in a prose that has now reached an acme of rarefied intensity:

"Not yet so much as this morning had she felt herself sink into possession; gratefully glad that the warmth of the southern summer was still in the high, florid rooms, palatial chambers where hard, cool pavements took reflections in their lifelong polish, and where the sun on the stirred sea-water, flickering up through open windows, played over the painted 'subjects' in the splendid ceilings—medallions of purple and brown, of brave old melancholy colour, medals as of reddened gold, embossed and be-ribboned, all toned with time and all flourished and scolloped and gilded about, set in their great moulded and figured concavity (a nest of white cherubs, friendly creatures of the air) . . ." (page 282)

She has used her wealth to counter-attack her destiny, to live. "One can't do more than live," she says to Lord Mark shortly before she dies. In order to live, she has chosen the most precious treasure civilization can offer her, a palace where enclosure does not mean imprisonment but freedom:

"She insisted that her palace—with all its romance and art and history—had set up round her a whirlwind of suggestion that never dropped for an hour. It wasn't therefore, within such walls, confinement, it was the freedom of all the centuries." (page 309)

Milly can leave outside the palace the necessities of life, its intrigues and betrayals, and also the passions of life—the conditions that Merton Densher imposes on Kate Croy in order to continue plotting their dreary planning[21]—symbolized in that Venice "all of evil", "profaned and bewildered by some reverse of fortune", lashed by rain.

Milly has chosen her "ark", which could save her from the deluge, reconstructing a "court", more than once compared—in its composition and characters—to a painting by Veronese[22]. With the creation of

Palazzo Leporelli, James pays the ultimate homage to the city of art—Venice, but also, in a wider sense, to his own world, the world of art, his own fortress—showing that one can do more than just live: *write*. Milly's—and James's—palace, which had found its "germ" in his impressions of Palazzo Barbaro, now has a literary reality, independent of real life.

When the novel was finished, and the past exorcised, James could leave behind also the "germ", or the "model" which he had used to build his own Palazzo Leporelli. This is clear in James's letter to Alvin L. Coburn, the artist who was to photograph the places of James's fiction for the New York Edition (1907–09). In James's letter (**XXVII**) it is quite clear that Palazzo Barbaro no longer had a great importance in relation to Palazzo Leporelli. James wrote to Coburn that he had had Palazzo Barbaro "vaguely" in mind, an affirmation quite obviously "false" as regards the genesis of Palazzo Leporelli, but quite "true" in 1907, when—to illustrate the meaning of the novel—a "sort of symbolised and generalised Venice" would be just as appropriate.

James also gave Coburn some directions on the possible perspectives from which to photograph Palazzo Barbaro, but he quickly advised Coburn to use "some other palace" if none of these perspectives "yielded something" Coburn felt was "effective". The main thing was to have an "effective" image, rendering the quintessence of Venice in its "noble and fine aspect" rather than in its "shabby and familiar" mode. James wanted Coburn to catch and express that sense of history—and art—which Palazzo Leporelli held in "its great lap", that past civilization which "the ghost of old Daniele" [Barbaro] and the other great humanists of the family, had contributed to the city. These were figures who were now only ghosts, but whose voices the writer evoked in the Preface to *A London Life*, in 1908:

"[I] remember in fact beginning it [*A London Life*], in one of the wonderful faded back rooms of an old Venetian palace, a room with a pompous Tiepolo ceiling and walls of ancient pale-green damask, slightly shredded and patched, which, on the warm mornings, looked into the shade of a court where a high outer staircase, strikingly bold, yet strikingly relaxed, held together one scarce knew how; where Gothic windows broke out, on discoloured blanks of wall, at quite arbitrary levels, and where above all the strong Venetian voice, full of history and humanity and waking perpetual echoes, seemed to say more in ten warm words, of whatever tone, than any twenty pages of one's cold prose."[23]

JAMES AND *THE ASPERN PAPERS*

These letters tell us the story of the relationship of the writer with the city and with one of its most splendid palaces, opening new perspectives and showing us the way in which the imagination of a great writer works in the process of transforming impressions of reality into the more real life of fiction. But these letters of course also tell us much about James's everyday life and contacts.

They tell us, for example, about the characters of that "queer, polyglot, promiscuous society" which James frequented both in Florence and in Venice— but also in London and in Paris, a society that seems to weigh more and more on the writer as the years go by, as it eroded time from his writing. But even among these characters belonging to a glittering, often frivolous world, which always liked to have some royalty in its set, be it a pretender or an exiled king, James did manage to find some true friends and some "germs" for his fiction. Even in the most frivolous and mundane conversation, James could suddenly find a trifle, a glittering ice shard that opened up his imagination.

It was in fact in Florentine society—described at length and compared to that of Venice (III, IV)—that James first heard the story of Byron's letters, some of which Countess Gamba, who had inherited them from Teresa Gamba Guiccioli, managed to burn[24]. This was a story that attracted James's imagination, always alert both to the precious value of any "paper" written by a great poet and to the necessity to preserve the privacy of the writer—as his burning of so many of his own papers shows. The Venetian setting where James transferred the story of Jeffrey Aspern's papers, in *The Aspern Papers* (1888), a short novel which is also a psychological thriller, testifies to James's conscious use of the tradition of the representation of Venice. In the devious and secret Venice of *The Aspern Papers*, James used the traditional Anglo-Saxon representation of the city as an attractive and at the same time dangerously alluring place, according to the tradition created by Nash and Shakespeare, Radcliffe and Cooper, and in some measure, by Byron himself.[25]

In *The Aspern Papers* this representation of Venice was masterfully deprived of its exterior gothic features and became the objective correlative of psychological states and pursuits. The labyrinthine alleys of the city are the echoing mirror of the labyrinths of the mind, of the devious purposes of the character who wants to lay his hands on Jeffrey Aspern's letters, and of the owner of the letters, Juliana, who holds on to them with just as secret and devious a plotting, ready to release the letters only under her own unacceptable conditions.

But in *The Aspern Papers* one can also perceive an echo of James's notes on the poverty and the decadence of the city, after Napoleon's plundering. The great barren hall of the palace where Juliana and Tita live is the real and symbolic entrance to the treasure room where Juliana, even on the threshold of death, stands her guard and catches the "publishing scoundrel" red-handed; it is also a strong image of a city robbed of its treasures, where everything has its price, where everything can be bought: Tiepolo ceilings, rococo chairs, whole family archives. In this world of moral and material decadence, money—the enormous amount of money Juliana asks her guest as rent for a few, empty rooms—buys hospitality. In James's world, where so many exchanges involving money, concern works of art, there can be an even more radical—and blackmailing—exchange: marriage. The society of antique dealers, the various Carrers and Richettis and Riettis who sold everything they could find, laying waste whole palaces, seems to be governed by very simple economic rules, in a sort of rough innocence, as compared with the complex plots of buying and selling that go on in *The Aspern Papers.*

JAMES AND SOCIETY

An episode that James heard in a Florentine salon gave birth to a small and perfect masterpiece.

Characters glimpsed during a tea party or an elegant dinner offered the "germs" for possible new characters in fiction. In Venice, Princess Olga of Montenegro, the daughter of Queen Darinka, the widow of the assassinated King of Montenegro, "the poor little princess with no money or art" became "a possible subject, needing to be a little filled out".[26]

The royal wealth of Isabella Stewart Gardner, with her black clothes made by the Parisian designer Worth, and her famous, long, long string of perfect pearls, who together with the Countess Pisani reminded James of the romantic heroines of English novels (IV), became possible "germs" for the sublime character of Milly Theale. Good Mrs. Bronson, Browning's friend in the last years of the poet's life, suggested to James the character of Mrs. Prest in *The Aspern Papers*. James pondered at length on Browning himself as a possible character for a story.[27]

James had an ambivalent attitude to the society in which he lived, typified by his attitude to Isabella Stewart Gardner ("Mrs. Jack"). How can one forget the portrait of this rich and powerful lady, in the habit of commanding people, whom James addressed in a half-joking and half-affectionate tone? (II, X, XVI,

XXIII.) In one letter (II), James presented himself as a 'ruminant quadruped', one of the patient beasts always ready to pull her "triumphant car" or "tow" her gondola. But James's humorous tone does not hide a basic criticism of that "Mrs. Jack", who has everything, does everything, in her "preposterously pleasant career", as a collector of the spoils of Europe.

James tried to defend himself from Mrs. Gardner's hectic life. "How she must be flashing, or at any rate splashing, at the Barbaro!"[28] he wrote to Mr. Curtis in 1897, when Mrs. Gardner had taken temporary possession of the Palazzo Barbaro. The "divine stillness" of the palace "spinned around" when the "little lady" lived in it. In 1893 James wrote to Isabella that he could imagine her at the Chicago Exhibition, with her own palace, "an infinitely more barbarous Barbaro",[29] on the top floor of which he would like to have a "small marble hall with thirteen curtains and a pink mosquito net". Only on these conditions will he go, on no other. The little lady always on the move, busy buying Titians, Mantegnas and Vermeers, rococo chairs and *cuori d'oro* (golden leather hangings embossed with gold) did in fact build her own palace, a little "more barbarous" than the Barbaro. The wonderful Fenway Court, in Boston, became her own imagined and real Palazzo Leporelli.[30]

Many other characters appear in these letters. Henry's brother William and their sister Alice, with whom the writer spent some time in Venice, apparently not very happily, because of the many famished mosquitoes. There are James's American friends living in Italy: Francis Boott, the musician, and his daughter Lizzie, married to the painter Frank Duveneck; Aunt Kate, the sister of James's mother, and other lady friends, such as Grace Norton, Sarah Butler Wister, and after 1899, the English Miss Jessie Allen. As the letters indicate, with some of these people, at first worldly *conoscenze*, a relation of deep friendship developed over the years, especially with the Curtises and Miss Allen.

A society of expatriates in love with Italy gradually takes shape, sprinkled here and there with exiled emperors and princes, or with visiting royalty, mixing with the few surviving members of the Venetian patrician class who had escaped ruin (not unlike the society of Venice of the present *fin de siècle*). This society mixes with artists, poets, writers, musicians (as it still does). In the letters we are given glimpses of this world that struck James as "a vain agitation of insignificant particles",[31] but in whose ceremonies and rites he himself participated.

The Curtises, Daniel and Ariana, are in a way the

exemplary representatives of this world, in their exquisite palace, where:

"The cosmopolite habit, the modern sympathy, the intelligent flexible attitude, the latest fruit of time, adjust themselves to the great gilded, relinquished shell and try to fill it out."

Because, James adds:

"A Venetian palace that has not too grossly suffered and that is not overwhelming by its mass makes almost any life graceful that may be led in it."[32]

The Curtises, like so many other members of this cosmopolitan society, take tea with the Queen of Montenegro, sitting in a circle in front of a blinding lamp, surrounded by portraits of the royal family in their Montenegro costumes. They dine at the Layards', at Palazzo Cappello on the Grand Canal, where the former ambassador and discoverer of Niniveh has his splendid collection of Italian paintings, among them Bellini's *Mahomet II*, bought with the help of Giovanni Morelli[33], and where Lady Layard wears a necklace made of the Mesopotamian seals found by her husband. They receive their "neighbour", Countess Pisani, who lives in the same palace when she is not in the country looking after her farm. In their palazzo, Robert Browning reads his poems to a group of friends, after spending the morning on the Lido, walking along the beach, and returning, with Daniel and Ariana, in their gondola. They also take part in other society rituals that have now disappeared: the evenings of the *tableaux vivants*, where Ariana is a Van Dyck and a young Mocenigo girl is a Titian, while the "director", the painter Duveneck, is a "bravo of Venice", romantically menacing. Ariana's letter on the *tableaux vivants* gives us a glimpse of a social rite which appears in Edith Wharton's *The House of Mirth*?[34]

The Curtises are part of the group of expatriate Americans, just like Mrs. Bronson, who has learnt Italian but especially the Venetian dialect so well that she can write *commediette* in this dialect and stage them at home, with "monstrously clever" young players.[35] These expatriates have, however, a strong animosity towards their motherland that James does not share, as he underlines in one letter (IX). To look for the possible causes of this animosity, one finds an episode where causes and effects are totally disproportionate. The Curtises seem to have left Boston—for ever—due to an offence. The story goes that Daniel climbed onto a streetcar, and finding his usual seat taken by a gentleman who did not stand up to vacate the seat, quarrelled with him, pinching his nose.[36]

Unfortunately the man was Judge Churchill, who took him to court. Mr. Curtis was sentenced to pay a fine or to spend one night in prison. He chose to leave Boston for ever. But there are other versions of the story, some more favourable to Mr. Curtis, such as the one where the quarrel is said to have originated with the judge not allowing a pregnant woman to sit in Mr. Curtis's usual seat.

Perhaps in reality, the Curtises, just like so many other expatriates, were looking for a less rigid way of life, a softer life—not only in terms of the climate—which allowed them to enjoy art and culture without the sudden frosts of the New England Puritan tradition.

This world is present in James's letters, but also in the letters of the Curtises, which cannot—and must not—be compared with the wonderful writing in James's letters. We present here some unpublished letters by Daniel and Ariana to Daniel's sister, Mary, because these letters too offer curious glimpses of that strange "garden of social flowers" which was the Anglo-Venetian society of that epoch. These are family letters that also tell—insisting on secrecy!—of the hoped-for purchase of Palazzo Barbaro (III), of the objects bought at an auction to embellish it, and of the secret staircase that has been discovered in the palace (IV). Together with Ariana's notes, written in 1908, in a quick summarizing perspective, these letters not only give information on the people who frequented the Barbaro, but also on the restoration of the palace.

The quiet and familiar letters of Daniel and Ariana are followed by those of their son Ralph, the painter, all addressed to Isabella Stewart Gardner, sparkling with vivacious news and suggestions. Ralph's is an intense *fin de siècle* life, with endless travelling between Paris and London, Marienbad and the Côte d'Azur (where he had a villa), Spain and Germany, for art and music, but also for hunts and dances and thermal cures, or to hear Wagner's *Tristan* in Bayreuth. Ralph seems to live intensely, to want to enjoy life quickly, at all costs, while there is time. Ralph's letters seem to foresee that the world in which Daniel and Ariana live peacefully, imagining it will last for ever, will come to an abrupt and tragic end. In May 1914 Ralph Curtis, writing to Isabella Stewart Gardner, still declares that everything is going on as usual, that there is nothing new; but in the following letter, dated September 2, 1915, in the midst of war, everything has inexorably changed. The description of Venice, seen as a "primadonna in mourning", with all its hotels and shops closed, the golden angels covered with grey sackcloth, seems to place the final seal on the brilliant personal life of Ralph and on the more general history of a whole society. The sense is of an ending: the very sense that James expressed in a letter to Jessie Allen in 1907, beneath the discursive, even gossipy surface, James must tell Miss Allen "of the new heartbreak it is to feel this enchantress (I allude now to the terrible old Venice herself!) weave her spell just again supremely to lose her".

The different destinies of Henry James, the Curtises, the gilded *fin de siècle* world, merge in the destruction of World War I.

After another war, a little girl climbed "the strikingly bold, yet strikingly relaxed" open staircase of the Palazzo Barbaro: the granddaughter of Ralph took her place in the palace. Her memoir, at the end of this book, gives us a glimpse of a palace that has survived Napoleonic plunders and spoliation, ruin and wars, to continue the tradition of art, history, and of civilization into the next century.

NOTES

1. Poliziano (Angelo Ambrogini called il Poliziano, 1454–1494), the Florentine humanist, famous for his Greek and Latin studies, for his translations and his poetry. His masterpiece is the poem *Stanze per la giostra* (1494) written to celebrate the young Giuliano de' Medici's victory in a tournament, and interrupted because of the young prince's death.

2. On the Barbaros, see M.L. King, *Venetian Humanism in an Age of Patrician Dominance*, Princeton, Princeton University Press, 1986; V. Branca, *Poliziano e l'umanesimo della parola*, Turin, Einaudi, 1983 and *La sapienza civile*, Florence, Olschki 1998; M. Tafuri, *Venezia e il Rinascimento*, Turin, Einaudi 1985; *Una famiglia veneziana nella storia. I Barbaro*, eds. M Marangoni, M. Pastore Stocchi, Venice, Istituto Veneto di Scienze, Lettere ed Arti, 1996. On Marc Antonio Barbaro see the entry by F. Gaeta, in *Dizionario Biografico degli Italiani*, VI, 1964, pp.110–112. On Francesco Barbaro, Marc'Antonio's oldest son and the successor of Giovanni Grimani in the patriarchate of Aquileia, a figure of great importance in the Counter-Reformation, see the entry by G. Benzoni in *Dizionario Biografico degli Italiani*, VI, pp.104–106; G. Trebbi, *Francesco Barbaro patrizio veneto e patriarca d'Aquileia*, Udine, Casamassima, 1984. On Antonio Barbaro, the entry by G. Benzoni in *Dizionario Biografico degli Italiani*, VI, pp.86–89. On Napoleon's devastations and more generally on XIX century plunders see A. Zorzi, *Venezia scomparsa*, Milan, Electa, 1984 (1972), and *Venezia austriaca*, Bari, Laterza, 1985. On the dispersals of archives and libraries see M. Zorzi, *La Libreria di San Marco*, Milan, Mondadori, 1987.

3. From an unpublished anonymous diary, a ms. of the Biblioteca Nazionale Marciana, in course of publication. The diary is Daniel Curtis's. See Rosella Mamoli Zorzi, "Henry

James in a 'Venetian' Diary", in *Henry James Review*, 11, 1990, pp.101–114.

4. The great ceiling canvas, the so-called *Apotheosis of Francesco Barbaro* is now at the Metropolitan Museum of New York. It was in fact sold in 1866, before the palace was bought by the Curtises and therefore before James was a guest of the Curtises, although the writer seems to have considered the "pompous Tiepolo ceiling" the real thing. The other Tiepolos, the ovals in the great salon, *The Offering to Juno Lucana*, *The Betrothal of Alexander and Roxana*, *The Death of Arsinoe*, *Tarquinius and Lucretia*, were sold in 1874 and are now respectively in Pavia, Copenhagen, Washington, Augsburg; see M. Gemin, F. Pedrocco, *Giambattista Tiepolo. Dipinti*, Venice, Arsenale, 1993. See n. 16, p.211 and Ariana Curtis's Notes, unpublished ms. of the Biblioteca Nazionale Marciana, published here in the original English version for the first time. On Palazzo Barbaro see G. J. Fontana, *Cento palazzi di Venezia storicamente illustrati*, Venice, Scarabellini, 1934 (1850), pp.119–122; E. Bassi, *Palazzi di Venezia*, Venice, La Stamperia, 1976, pp.57, 325, 512; P. Lauritzen and A. Zielcke, *Palaces of Venice*, Florence, Becocci, 1978, pp.102–107, and obviously John Ruskin, *The Stones of Venice*, in *The Complete Works of John Ruskin*, ed. by E. T. Cook and A. Wedderburn, London, Allen, 1904, vol. XI, bk. 3 of *The Stones*.

5. Ruskin helped Alvise Piero Zorzi to publish his *Osservazioni intorno ai restauri interni ed esterni della Basilica di San Marco*, Venice, Ongania, 1877 (reprinted in: Dalla Costa, *La Basilica di San Marco e i restauri dell'Ottocento*, Venice, La Stamperia di Venezia, 1983). On the subject see also J. Clegg, *Ruskin and Venice*, London, Junction Books, 1981.

6. *An Interior in Venice*, in P. Hills, *John Singer Sargent*, New York, Whitney, 1987, p.69 (n. 44) and in the catalogue *Venezia*

nell'Ottocento, edited by G. Pavanello and G. Romanelli, Venice, Electa, 1983, pp.209–210. The painting is at the Royal Academy in London. *Mrs. Gardner in Venice* (1894) by Anders Zorn is at the Isabella Stewart Gardner Museum in Boston. *The Barbaro Palace* by Walter Gay is at the Boston Museum of Fine Arts and is published in W. Gay, *Paintings of French Interiors*, edited by A.E. Gallatin, New York, Dutton, 1920, n. 15. F. Latimer's paintings are in a private collection.

7. Letters will be indicated in this introduction with the number they are marked with in this edition, in parenthesis.

8. *The Grand Canal*, in *Italian Hours*, New York, Grove Press, p.39.

9. See the photograph of the canopied bed, in the Isabella Stewart Gardner Museum collection in Boston.

10. Henry James, *Letters, 1843–1875*, vol. I, edited by Leon Edel, London, Macmillan, 1974, p.134, letter of September 21, 1869 to John La Farge. The reference to James's letters will be shortened to "Edel, *Letters*" hereafter.

11. On the relation with Ruskin, see Leon Edel's volumes, in particular *The Untried Years* (1843–1870), New York, Discus, 1978; J. Clegg, "Superficial Pastimes, fine emotions and metaphysical intentions: James and Ruskin in Venice", in *Henry James e Venezia*, edited by S. Perosa, Florence, Olschki, 1987. On Tintoretto's and James's mannerism, see B. and G. Melchiori, *Il gusto di Henry James*, Turin, Einaudi, 1974; L. Lepschy, *Tintoretto Observed*, Ravenna, Longo, 1983; Rosella Mamoli Zorzi, "Tintoretto e gli Anglo-Americani," in *Annali di Ca' Foscari*, XXXV, 1–2, 1996. On James and Venice see Leon Edel's volumes, *The Untried Years cit.*, *The Conquest of London*, *The Middle Years*, *The Treacherous Years*, *The Master*, all New York, Discus, 1978. Among studies entirely devoted to this topic,

see M. Battilana, *Venezia sfondo e simbolo nella narrativa di Henry James*, Milan, Laboratorio delle arti, 1987 (1971). See also *The Sweetest Impression of Life, The James Family and Italy*, edited by A. Lombardo and J. W. Tuttleton, New York and Rome, New York University Press and Istituto dell'Enciclopedia Italiana, 1990, and T. Tanner, *Venice Desired*, Cambridge, Harvard University Press, 1992.

12. As regards composition, one should look at the passage on the San Rocco *Crucifixion* in the Preface to *The Tragic Muse*, in *Henry James, Literary Criticism, French Writers, Other European Writers, The Prefaces to the New York Edition*, edited by Leon Edel, with the assistance of M. Wilson, New York, The Library of America, 1984, p.1107.

13. Edel, *Utters, I*, p.160.

14. On Constance Woolson see Edel, *The Middle Years cit.*, *The Master cit.* On January 25, 1894, the *Gazzetta di Venezia* announced the death of the American writer. James Fenimore Cooper was the author of *The Leatherstocking Tales*, among which is *The Last of the Mohicans*.

15. Letter to Mrs. Curtis from Casa Biondetti (1894). Dartmouth College Library, Curtis Correspondence.

16. See Alide Cagidemetrio, *Black Balloons and White Doves*, in *Henry James e Venezia* cit.

17. Unpublished manuscript by Zina Hulton, *Fifty Years in Venice*, p.103, Ashmolean Museum, Oxford.

18. Edel, *The Master* cit., pp.109–110.

19. On the evolution of James's narrative strategies see S. Perosa, *Henry James and the Experimental Form*, New York, New York University Press, 1980.

20. *The Wings of the Dove*, Penguin Modern Classics, 1965, p.292. Subsequent page references to this novel will be printed in the text.

21. See T. Tanner, *op. cit.*, on Eros and Venice.

22. On the identification and the function of the Veronese painting (*The Queen of Sheba in front of Solomon*, now attributed to Veronese's workshop) see J. Clegg, *art.cit.*, p.163. On the relationship between narrative and pictorial techniques, also as regards Veronese, V. Hopkins, *Henry James and the Visual Arts*, Charlottesville, The University of Virginia Press, 1970, pp.84–85.

23. *Prefaces* cit., p.1152.

24. See also *The Complete Notebooks of Henry James*, edited by Leon Edel and L. H. Powers, New York, Oxford University Press, 1987, p.34, and the *Preface* to *The Aspern Papers*, in *Literary Criticism* cit., pp.1173–1179 for the reference to Claire Clairmont and Shelley.

25. James used the letters of William Wetmore Story to evoke the gothic representation of Venice, see *William Wetmore Story and His Friends*, London, Thames and Hudson, volume 1, 1903, pages 118–9.

26. Letter to the Curtises, September 25 (no year) from Rye (Dartmouth, Curtis Correspondence).

27. See also James's notes on "the C. F. and Katrina B. subject", deriving from a conversation between Katherine Bronson and Constance Fletcher (in the *Notebooks* cit., p.208 and p.126). James eventually "used" the figure of Browning in the story *The Private Life* (1892) *(Notebooks*, p.60).

28. Letter to Mr. Curtis, August 1897, Dartmouth, Curtis Correspondence.

29. Letter to Isabella Stewart Gardner, Isabella Stewart Gardner Museum.

30. On Mrs. Gardner see M. Carter, *Isabella Stewart Gardner and Fenway Court*, Boston, Isabella Stewart Gardner Museum, 1925; L. Hall Tharp, *Mrs. Jack, A Biography*, New York, Congdon and Weed, 1965; *The Letters of Bernard Berenson and Isabella Stewart Gardner 1887–1924, with Correspondence by Mary Berenson*, edited by R. van N. Hadley, Boston, Northeastern University Press, 1987.

31. Edel, *Letters III*, p.169.

32. *The Grand Canal* cit., p.39.

33. Giovanni Morelli (1816–1891), Italian art critic, the author of many critical works on art, which he published in German, and the inventor of a method based on the identification of particular motifs *(motivi sigla)* which led to the attribution of paintings to the hand of a specific artist.

34. In this scene, often discussed by critics, there is a "Titian's daughter", a Van Dyck where a lady wears a black silk dress (like Ariana). Miss Bart is Reynolds's *Mrs. Lloyd*, although she had originally thought of being Tiepolo's *Cleopatra*. As Wharton wrote: "To an unfurnished mind *(tableaux vivants)* remain . . . only a superior kind of wax-works; but to the responsive fancy they may give magic glimpses of the boundary world between fact and imagination." *(The House of Mirth*, Penguin, p.133).

35. Ralph Curtis wrote to Mrs. Gardner, on April 13 (1894) on the back of a printed programme announcing *Un inglese a Venezia. La vigilia di San Martino* (An Englishman in Venice. The Vigil of San Martino), a *commedietta* (short play) in two acts by K. de KB. (Programme at the Isabella Stewart Gardner Museum). Incredible as it may seem, Mrs. Bronson had in fact learnt the

Venetian dialect well enough to write plays. The children who played in Mrs. Bronson's performances came from a school she had organized for the local inhabitants, whose poverty had upset her.

36. Daniel was thus given the nickname of "Pinchnose Curtis". This episode is part of Boston's oral history, but it is also recorded in L. Tharp, *op.cit.*, p.101.

The entrance, Palazzo Barbaro

LETTERS BY HENRY JAMES

I

To William James[1]
September 25*th* [1869]   Venice, Hotel Barbesi[2]
(Edel I)

My dear Bill –

I wrote to father as soon as I arrived here and
mentioned my intention of sending you some copious
account of my impressions of Venice. I have since
then written to J. La Farge[3] (briefly) and to Howells[4]
and worked off in some degree the *éblouissement* of the
first few days. I have a vague idea that I may write
some notes for the *Atlantic* or the *Nation*; but at the risk
of knocking the bottom out of them, I feel that I must
despatch you a few choice remarks—although I'm
too tired to plunge deeply into things. [. . .] I have
now been here nearly two weeks and have experienced
that inevitable reconciliation to things which six
months of Europe cause to operate so rapidly and
smoothly, no matter what the strangeness of things
may be. A little stare—a little thrill—a little curiosity,
and then all is over. You subside into the plodding

blasé, homesick "doer" of cities. Venice is magnificently fair and quite, to my perception, the Venice of Romance and fancy. Taine,[5] I remember, somewhere speaks of "Venice and Oxford—the two most picturesque cities in Europe." I personally prefer Oxford; it told me deeper and richer things than any I have learned here. It's as if I had been born in Boston: I can't for my life frankly surrender myself to the Genius of Italy, or the Spirit of the South—or whatever one may call the confounded thing; but I nevertheless *feel* it in all my pulses. If I could only write as I might talk I should have no end of things to tell you about my last days in Switzerland and especially my descent of the Alps—that mighty summer's day upon the Simplon when I communed with immensity and sniffed Italy from afar. This Italian tone of things which I then detected, lies richly on my soul and gathers increasing weight, but it lies as a cold and foreign mass—never to be absorbed and appropriated. The meaning of this superb image is that I feel I shall never look at Italy—at Venice, for instance—but from without; whereas it seemed to me at Oxford and in England generally that I was breathing the air of home. Ruskin[6] recommends the traveller to frequent and linger in a certain glorious room at the Ducal Palace, where P. Veronese revels on the ceilings and Tintoret rages[7] on the walls, because he "nowhere else will enter so deeply into the heart of Venice." But I feel as if I might sit there forever (as I sat there a long time this morning) and only feel more and more my inexorable Yankeehood. As a puling pining Yankee, however, I enjoy things deeply. What you will care most to hear about is the painters; so I shall not feel bound to inflict upon you any tall writing about the canals and palaces; the more especially as with regard to them, photographs are worth something; but with regard to the pictures comparatively nothing—*rapport à la couleur*—which is quite half of Venetian painting. The first thing that strikes you, when you come to sum up, after you've been to the Ducal Palace and the Academy, is that you have not half so much been seeing paintings as *painters*. The accumulated mass of works by a few men drives each man home to your senses with extraordinary force. This is especially the case with the greatest of them all—Tintoretto—so much so that he ends by becoming an immense perpetual moral presence, brooding over the scene and worrying the mind into some species of response and acknowledgement. I have had more eyes and more thoughts for him than for anything else in Venice; and in future, I fancy, when I recall the place, I shall remember chiefly the full-streaming, dazzling light of the heavens, and Tintoretto's dark range of color. Ruskin truly says that it is well to devote yourself here solely to three men—P. Veronese, Tintoretto and J. Bellini;[8] inasmuch as you can see sufficient specimens of the rest (including Italian) amply elsewhere but must come here for even a notion of these. This is true of the three, but especially of Tintoretto—whom I finally see there is nothing for me to do but to admit (and have done with it) to be the biggest genius (as far as I yet know) who ever wielded a brush. Once do this, and you can make your abatements; but if Shakespeare is the greatest of poets Tintoretto is assuredly the greatest of painters. He belongs to the same family and produces very much the same effect. He seems to me to have seen into painting to a distance unsuspected by any of his fellows: I don't mean into its sentimental virtues or didactic properties but into its simple pictorial capacity. Imagine Doré[9] a thousand times refined in quality and then as many times multiplied in quantity and you may have a sort of notion of him. But you must see him here at work like a great wholesale decorator to form an idea of his boundless invention and his passionate energy and the extraordinary possibilities of color—for he begins by striking you as the poorest and ends by impressing you as the greatest of colorists. Beside him the others are the simplest fellows in the world. For the present I give up Titian altogether. He is not adequately represented here. His *Assumption*[10] strikes me as a magnificent second-rate picture; his presentation of the Virgin is utterly killed by another of Tintoretto's. I fancy you must see him in England, Madrid etc. P. Veronese is really great, in a very simple fashion. He seems to have had in his head a perfect realization of a world in which all things were interfused with a sort of silvery splendor delicious to look upon. He is thoroughly undramatic and "impersonal". A splendid scene in the concrete was enough for him and when he paints anything of a story the whole action seems to rest suspended in order to look handsome and be painted. If I weren't a base Anglo-Saxon and a coward slave, I should ask nothing better than his *Rape of Europa* in the Doge's Palace where a great rosy blonde, gorgeous with brocade and pearls and bouncing with salubrity and a great mellow splendor of sea and sky and nymphs and flowers do their best to demoralize the world into a herd of Théophile Gautiers.[11] The great beauty of P. Veronese is the perfect unity and placidity of his talent. There is not a whit of struggle, nor fever, nor longing for the unattainable; simply a glorious sense of the look of things out of doors—of heads and columns against the sky, of the lustre of satin and of the beauty of looking up and seeing things lifted into the light above you. He is here chiefly found in the ceilings, where he is perfectly at home, and delights to force you to break your back to look at him—and wonder what sort of a back *he* must have had. John Bellini, a painter of whom I had no conception—one of the early Venetians—is equally great and simple in his own far different way. He has everything on a great scale—knowledge color and expression. He is the first "religious" painter I have yet seen who has made me understand that there can be—or that there once was at least, such a thing as pure religious art. I always fancied it more or less an illusion of the critics. But Bellini puts me to the blush. How to define his "religious" quality I know not; but he really makes you believe that his genius was essentially consecrated to heaven and that each of his pictures was a genuine act of worship. This is the more interesting because his piety prevails not the least against his science and his pictorial energy. There is not a ray in his works of debility or vagueness of conception. In vigor breadth and richness he is a thorough Venetian. His best pictures here possess an extraordinary perfection. Everything is equal—the full deep beauty of the expression—the masterly—the more than masterly firmness and purity of the drawing—and the undimmed, unfathomed lucidity and richness of the coloring. And then over it all the sort of pious deference has passed and hushed and smoothed and polished it till the effect is one of unspeakable purity. He has hardly more than one subject—the Virgin and Child, alone, or enthroned and attended with Saints and Cherubs; but you will be slow to tire of him, for long after you've had enough of his piety there is food for delight in the secret marvels of his handling. It gives me a strong sense of the vastness and strangeness of art, to compare these two men, Bellini and Tintoretto—to reflect upon their almost equal greatness and yet their immense dissimilarity, so that the great merit of each seems to have been that he possesses just these qualities the absence of which, apparently, ensures his high place to the other. But to return to Tintoretto. I'd give a great deal to be able to fling down a dozen of his pictures into prose of corresponding force and color. I strongly urge you to look up in vol. 3 of Ruskin's *Stones* (last appendix) a number of magnificent descriptive pages touching his principal pictures. (The whole appendix by the way, with all its exasperating points is invaluable to the visitor here and I have profited much by it.) I should be sadly at a loss to make you understand in what his great power consists—the more especially as he offers a hundred superficial points of repulsion to the well-regulated mind. In a certain occasional imbecility and crudity and imperfection of drawing Delacroix is nothing to him. And then you see him at a vast disadvantage inasmuch as with hardly an exception his pictures are atrociously hung and lighted. When you reflect that he was willing to go on covering canvas to be hidden out of sight or falsely shown, you get some idea of the prodigality of his genius. Most of his pictures are immense and swarming with figures; all have suffered grievously from abuse and neglect. But there are all sorts; you can never feel that you have seen the last; and each new one throws a new light on his resources. Besides this, they are extremely unequal and it would be an easy task I fancy to collect a dozen pieces which would conclusively establish him an unmitigated bore. His especial greatness, I should be tempted to say lies in the fact that more than any painter yet, he habitually conceived his subject as an *actual scene* which could not possibly have happened otherwise; not as a mere subject and fiction—but as a great fragment wrenched out of life and history, with all its natural details clinging to it and testifying to its reality. You seem not only to look *at* his pictures, but *into* them,—and this in spite of his not hesitating to open the clouds and shower down the deities and mix up heaven and earth as freely as his purpose demands. His *Miracle of St. Mark*[12] is a tremendous work, with life enough in it to animate a planet. But they can all paint a crowd, and this is as much Venetian as individual. A better specimen of his peculiar power is a simple *Adam and Eve*, in the same room or a *Cain and Abel*, its mate, both atrociously hung—away aloft in the air. Adam sits on a bank with his back to you; Eve facing you, with one arm wound round a tree leans forward and holds out the apple. The composition is so simple that it hardly exists and yet the painting is so rich and expressive that it seems as if the natural, the real, could go no further—unless indeed in the other, where Cain assaults Abel with an intent to kill more murderous and tragical than words can describe it. One of his works that has much struck me is a large *Annunciation*, immensely characteristic of this unlikeness to other painters. To the right sits the Virgin, starting back from her angelic visitant with magnificent surprise and terror. The Angel swoops down into the picture, leading a swarm of cherubs, not as in most cases where the subject is treated, as if he had come to pay her a pretty compliment but with a fury characteristic of his tremendous message. The greatest of all though—the greatest picture it seemed to me as I looked at it I ever saw—is a Crucifixion in a small church.[13] (He has treated the same subject elsewhere on a stupendous scale; but on the whole I prefer this.) Here, as usual, all is original and unconventional. Ruskin describes it far better than I can do.

Monday 26th. Having written so much last evening, I succumbed to slumber, and this evening I hardly feel like resuming the feeble thread of my discourse. I have been abroad all day bidding farewell to Venice, for I think of leaving tomorrow or next day. I began the day with several churches and saw two new and magnificent Tintorets and a beautiful Titian. Then I paid a farewell visit to the Academy, which I have got pretty well by heart—and where I saw Mr. and Mrs. Bronson[14] of Newport who knew me not—the latter very haggard and pale. After which I took a gondola over to the Lido to look my last at the Adriatic. It was a glorious afternoon and I wandered for nearly two hours by the side of the murmuring sea. I was more than ever struck with the resemblance of Venice—especially that part of it—to Newport. The same atmosphere, the same luminosity. Standing looking out at the Adriatic with the low-lying linked islands on the horizon was just like looking out to sea from one of the Newport beaches, with Narragansett afar. I have seen the Atlantic as blue and smooth and musical—almost! If words were not so stupid and colorless, *fratello mio*[15], and sentences so interminable and chirography so difficult, I should like to treat you to a dozen pages more about this watery paradise. Read Théophile Gautier's *Italia*; it's chiefly about Venice. I'm curious to know how this enchanted

fortnight will strike me, in memory ten years hence—
for altho' I've got absurdly used to it all, yet there
is a palpable sub-current of deep delight. Gondolas
spoil you for a return to common life. To begin with,
in themselves they afford the perfection of indolent
pleasure. The seat is so soft and deep and slumberous
and the motion so mild elastic and unbroken that
even if they bore you through miles of stupid darkness
you'd think it the most delectable fun. But when they
lift you thro' this rosy air, along these liquid paths,
beneath the balconies of palaces as lovely in design
and fancy as they are pathetic in their loneliness and
decay—you may imagine that it's better than walking
down Broadway. I should never have forgiven myself
had I come to Venice any later in the season. The
mosquitoes are perfectly infernal—and you can't
say more for Venice than that you are willing, at
this moment, for the sake of the days she bestows to
endure the nights she inflicts. But, bating this, all else
is in perfection—the weather, the temperature and
the aspect of the canals. The Venetian population,
on the water, is immensely picturesque. In the narrow
streets, the people are far too squalid and offensive to
the nostrils, but with a good breadth of canals to set
them off and a heavy stream of sunshine to light them
up as they go pushing and paddling and screaming—
bare-chested, bare-legged, magnificently tanned and

muscular—the men at least are a very effective lot. Besides lolling in my gondola I have spent a good deal of time in poking thro' the alleys which serve as streets and staring about in the *Campos*—the little squares formed about every church—some of them most sunnily desolate, the most grass-grown, the most cheerfully sad little reliquaries of a splendid past that you can imagine. Every one knows that the Grand Canal is a wonder; but really to feel in your heart the ancient wealth of Venice, you must have frequented these canalettos and campos and seen the number and splendor of the palaces that stand rotting and crumbling and abandoned to paupers.—If I might talk of these things I would talk of more and tell you in glowing accents how beautiful a thing this month in Italy has been and how my brain swarms with pictures and my bosom aches with memories. I should like in some neat formula to give you the *Italian feeling*—and tell you just how it is that one is conscious here of the aesthetic presence of the past. But you'll learn one day for yourself. You'll go to that admirable Verona and get your fill of it.—I wanted not only to say a hundred things about Tintoretto which I've left unsaid (indeed I've said nothing) but to gossip a bit about the other painters. Whether it is that the three great ones I've mentioned practically include all the rest or not, I can't say; but (with the exception of two or three primitive members of the school, especially Carpaccio, who seemed to have learned laboriously for themselves,) there flows from the great mass of the secondary fellows no very powerful emanation of genius. Immense aptitude and capital teaching—vigorous talent, in fine—seem to be the amount of the matter. In them the school trenches on vulgarity. Bonifazio, Caliari, the two Palmas, Paris Bordone etc. have all an immense amount of ability, (often of a very exquisite kind) to a comparatively small amount of originality. Nevertheless I'm very willing to believe—in fact I'm quite sure—that seen in other places, in detached examples each of them would impress and charm you very much as their betters do here. All of them know endless things about colour: in this they are indeed exquisite. Bonifazio is a somewhat coarser Titian—a perfect Monarch of the mellow and glowing and richly darksome. Paris Bordone equals him, on a slightly different range. C. Caliari (son of P. Veronese) is a very handsome imitation of his father—and if the latter's works were destroyed, we'd vote him a great master. But what has fascinated me most here after Tintoretto and Co. are the two great buildings—the Ducal Palace and St. Mark's church. You have a general notion of what they amount to; it's all you can have, until you see them. St. Marks, within, is a great hoary shadowy

tabernacle of mosaic and marble, entrancing you with its remoteness, its picturesqueness and its chiaroscuro—an immense piece of Romanticism. But the Ducal Palace is as pure and perpetual as the façade of the Parthenon—and I think of all things in Venice, it's the one I should have been gladdest to achieve—the one most worthy of civic affection and gratitude. When you're heated and weary to death with Tintoretto and his feverish Bible Stories, you can come out on the great Piazzetta, between the marble columns, and grow comparatively cool and comfortable with gazing on this work of art which has so little to do with *persons*! But I too am weary and hot—tho' I expect to find on my couch but little of coolness or comfort. I have the delightful choices of sleeping with my window open and being *devoured*— maddened, poisoned—or closing it, in spite of the heat, and being stifled! (I have made no allusion to the contents of Mother's letter, which I none the less prize. . . . But I must say good-night. I mean to write you again in a few days—*Not* about painters.
À toi

H. James jr.

NOTES

1. William James (1842–1910), James's oldest brother, a professor at Harvard. A famous pragmatist philosopher and psychologist, he was the author of many important studies, among which *Principles of Psychology* (1890), *The Will to Believe* (1897), *The Varieties of Religious Experience* (1907). His *Correspondence* is also of the greatest interest.

2. Hotel Barbesi was at San Samuele, on the Grand Canal, with annexed bathing facilities.

3. John La Farge (1835–1910), the American painter. He gave painting lessons to Henry and William at Newport in 1860–1862 and greatly influenced Henry, also through the choice of readings he advised him on.

4. William Dean Howells (1837–1920), the American writer and critic, the champion of "genteel" realism in the U.S., extremely influential in the field of literature.

5. Hippolyte Adolphe Taine (1828–1893), the French writer and critic, whose *Italy, Rome and Naples*, James had reviewed in 1868.

6. "The traveller who really loves painting ought to get leave to come to this room whenever he chooses; and should pass the summer sunny mornings there again and again, wandering now and then in the Anti-Collegio, and Sala dei Pregadi, and coming back to rest under the wings of the crouched lion at the feet of the "Mocenigo". He will not otherwise enter so deeply into the heart of Venice" in *The Complete Works of John Ruskin cit.*, vol. XI, p.376. The second reference (to the three artists one should see in Venice) is on p.359. The description of Tintoretto's San Cassiano *Crucifixion* is on pp.366–367. On Tintoretto

and English and American writers see Rosella Mamoli Zorzi, "Tintoretto e gli angloamericani nell'Ottocento", in *Annali di Ca' Foscari*, XXV, 1–2, 1996, pp.189–224, and Anna Laura Lepschy, *Tintoretto Observed*, Ravenna, Longo, 1983.

7. "Rages": James may have chosen this verb basing himself on Taine, or on the definition of Tintoret as "l'irato" (ira=rage) used in XIX century guidebooks. See Giulio Lecomte, *Venezia*, Cecchini, 1844, p.377 (". . . the passion of the one his contemporaries called il furioso, l'irato . . .") (my translation).

8. James clearly means Giovanni Bellini, and not Jacopo; moreover Giovanni is the third great painter named by Ruskin.

9. Gustave Doré (1832–1883). James loved this artist whose illustrations of Perrault's *Contes* and Dante's *Commedia* he had much appreciated as a child. He often referred to Doré even after 1900. See A. Tintner, *The Museum World of Henry James*, *Preface* by Leon Edel, Ann Arbour, UMI Research Press, 1986, pp.18–21.

10. Titian's *Assumption*, now in the Santa Maria Gloriosa dei Frari church, was at the time in the Accademia Gallery, where it remained until 1919. The hall, as it was, is represented in M. Moro and G. Brizeghel's lithograph, "The Hall of the Assumption in The Venice Academy", reproduced in *Venezia nell'Ottocento cit.*, p.129. *The Presentation of the Virgin* was, and still is, in its original place, i.e. the "Sala dell'Albergo" of the Scuola della Carità, now the Accademia Gallery. Tintoretto's *Presentation* is in the church of the Madonna dell'Orto.

11. James wrote several times on Gautier, whom he admired with some reservations, however, on his moral sense, as in this very passage. James found Gautier particularly clever in his descriptions of bodies: "Flesh and blood, noses and bosoms,

arms and legs were a delight to him, and it was his mission to dilate upon them", as he wrote in 1873 *(French Writers* in *Literary Criticism cit.*, p.367.)

12. At the Accademia Gallery, just as the *Adam and Eve* and *Cain and Abel*, which are however at eye level now, quite visible. Tintoretto's *Annunciation* is in the lower hall of the Scuola di San Rocco.

13. The church of San Cassiano (or San Cassano). This *Crucifixion* is described at length in *The Stones of Venice* by Ruskin, while the one in the Scuola di San Rocco has only two lines: "I must leave this picture to work its will on the spectator; for it is beyond all analysis, and above all praise" *(Venetian Index*, entry "Rocco, Scuola di").

14. Mr. and Mrs. Bronson: the American Katherine de Kay (1834–1901) married Arthur Bronson in 1855. Mr. Bronson died in Paris in 1885. From 1875 they lived in Europe, and Mrs. Bronson, from 1876, lived in Casa Alvisi, formerly a palazzo Giustinian, right across from the Salute church, on the Grand Canal. James was a guest at Casa Alvisi in 1887, and of Mrs. Bronson's house he wrote in the essay "Casa Alvisi" (1902). Mrs. Bronson's daughter, Edith, born in 1861, married Cosimo Rucellai, of the noble Florentine family, in 1895, and lived in Tuscany, where her mother died. On Mrs. Bronson see *More than Friend*, edited by M. Meredith and R. S. Humphrey, also on her friendship with Robert Browning (Armstrong Browning Library and Wedgestone Press, 1985).

15. "Brother of mine" in Italian.

II

To Isabella Stewart Gardner[1]
May *2nd* [1884]   3 Bolton St. Piccadilly
(I.S.G.M. Ms.)

Dear Mrs. Gardner –

I ought to have answered before this your terrible little letter from Agra—but you mentioned the 1st of May as the first moment, probably, at which you would find my own epistle (at Venice:) and I reflect that this is only May 2nd and that people never arrive in Venice as soon as they expect to. As you must have been dallying with the Orientals on the way, you probably won't get there for another week or so. I am myself, as you see, a striking example of the truth of that axiom—that one doesn't get to Venice as soon as one expected to the year before. I shall not get there for a long time, my dear lady—till a long time after you have left. I shall see you before that, here in London, and will then explain to you the source of my little delays. You will talk perhaps about broken vows—or you would, at least, if you were not a woman of infinite tact. We must break something, sometimes, and if I didn't smash a promise occasionally, I should fracture something more valuable still. I won't ask you to forgive me—for you will pretend you won't—even long after you have really done so—and the plea of extenuating circumstances sounds weak. I would much rather pose as a faithless friend—I so seldom have the opportunity. It is true that I haven't the excitement of believing that you miss me—on the lagoon—for I know too well that you don't miss any thing or any one in this preposterously pleasant career of yours. You have everything, you do everything, you enjoy everything, and if you don't happen to find an extra-post-horse at Venice to pull your triumphal car—to tow your gondola—you may be sure the poor patient beast will be waiting at the next *étape*. In other words I shall be waiting in London, and shall get into harness when you arrive. In the meanwhile have pity on the place where the collar has rubbed. I wear a collar always: *que dis-je?* I wear half a dozen. They are piled up round my poor old head, and when you see me you will scarce distinguish the tip of my nose. I am a ruminant quadruped, too, and I turn it over in my mind that, really, I, at least, am too good a friend of yours to lend a further hand—or hoof—in spoiling you. I have heard about the King of Cambodia—and the Nizam of Hyderabad (?)—about all your adventures and entertainments and I feel kind of savage at the thought that you have had this lovely time while I have had a rude workaday life, jolting and scraping from one dull day to the other. I don't pity you, dear lady—though I appreciate you as much as ever. I send you herein a line from Mrs. Bronson, who, however, is so absurdly easy to know that you will throw it overboard. Take it out of me here, and believe me ever yours unfaithfully,

Henry James

NOTE

1. Isabella Stewart Gardner (1840–1924), the famous collector and founder of the Isabella Stewart Gardner Museum at Fenway Court in Boston. Her extraordinary collection was put together mainly on the advice of Bernard Berenson. She arrived in Venice for the first time on May 13, 1884—later than planned, as James foresaw—coming from Constantinople by sea, after a long trip in the East. With Mr. Gardner, she had been received by two kings of Cambodia, she had been to China, and at Hyderabad, not finding any hotels, they had had to sleep in tent n.7 at the Public Gardens. This long trip had been made on the advice of Mrs. Gardner's doctor, after Mrs. Gardner had suffered from depression following the death of her child. Mrs. Gardner rented several times Palazzo Barbaro from the Curtises. Part of this letter was published by L. Hall Tharp, *op.cit.*, p.104.

III

To Grace Norton[1]
February 27*th* [1887]   Venice, Palazzino Alvisi
(Edel III)

My dear Grace.

Yesterday comes in your delightful letter of February 8th, following (at a shorter interval than I deserved), a most benevolent one of November 23d, which reached me in Florence shortly after I had written to you at Pisa. [. . .] I came to this place five days ago—after spending some ten weeks in Florence. I left England for six or eight—but it is now my hope that I may remain away till the summer. Alice[2] has kindly taken my rooms and servants off my hands and this simplifies the problems connected with an empty habitation and "Mr. and Mrs. Smith" (my domestics!) demoralized by the master's long absence. As I dislike the Season, in London, "worse and worse," I felicitate myself on escaping it this year. The first month I was in Florence I had a villa at Bellosguardo, kindly sublet to me by a friend (Constance Fenimore Woolson[3] the novelist—an excellent woman, of whom I am very fond, though she is almost impracticably deaf), who had taken it for three years and was not yet ready to go into it, having another on her hands. A cook went with it—a venerable—and veritable *chef*—so that I was very comfortable—and blissfully lifted out of that little simmering social pot—a not very savoury human broth—into which Florence resolves itself today. It is a pity it is *personally* so tiresome, for (allowing for the comparative ugliness of its winter phase, with hard cold and dusty *tramontana)* it had never seemed to me, naturally and artistically, more delightful. And the views from the villas on the hills (I was at a good many) are as beautiful—really—as your memory must tell you. On January 1st my friend came into her villa and I descended into Florence—where (I am told) I went "out" a good deal. Why, I don't know—as it was very exactly what I had left London not to do. I am also told I was "lionized"—and the wherefore of this I know still less. On reflection, in fact, I greatly doubt it. But I did see a great many people; too many, for what they were. I won't tell you their names, or more than that they were members of the queer, promiscuous polyglot (most polyglot in the world) Florentine society. The Russians are the great factor there and the two pleasantest houses are supposed to be that of Mme de Tchiatchef and that of the Marchesa Incontri. The former is a remarkably nice and sympathetic Englishwoman married to a rich and retired Russian diplomatist; the latter a singularly clever and easy Russian, (with a beautiful villa outside of Porta S. Gallo) who, divorced from her first husband, Prince Galitzin, married a Florentine and became his widow. Mme de T. is very good (and yet not dull) and Mme Incontri I suspect of being *bad*—though not dull either. The latter receives both the serious and the "smart" people, is literary (writes poorish novels, under false names, in English, which she speaks in absolute perfection) and also, I think, rather dangerous. The most intelligent person in Florence is Violet Paget[4] (Vernon Lee) who has lived there all her life, and receives every day, from 4 to 7, and as often in the evening as people will come to her. She is exceedingly ugly, not "well off," disputatious, contradictious and perverse; has a clever, paralysed half-brother, Edward Hamilton, formerly in diplomacy—who is always in her salon, bedridden or rather sofa-ridden—and also a grotesque, deformed, invalidical, *posing* little old mother, and a father in the highest degree unpleasant, mysterious and sinister, who walks *all day*, all over Florence, hates his stepson, and hasn't sat down to table with his family for twenty years. Yet in spite of these drawbacks, Miss Paget's intellectual and social energy are so great, that she attracts all the world to her drawing room, discusses all things in *any* language, and understands some, drives her pen, glares through her spectacles and keeps up her courage. She has a *mind*—almost the only one in Florence. I saw also something of a very clever, natural, exuberant Countess Gamba who is one of the figures of the place—niece by her husband of Byron's Guiccioli[5] (she has a lot of his letters to the G. which she declares shocking and unprintable—she took upon herself to burn one of them up!) and *putative* natural daughter of Giuseppe Giusti, the satiric Tuscan poet. (Her mother was some fine Florentine lady to whom G. was much devoted, and she—the "Euphrosyne"— is said much to resemble him.) She was the most of a "nature" of anyone I saw. I encountered no interesting man save [Adolf von] Hildebrand,[6] the admirable, original German sculptor, who has the feeling of the Greeks and that of the early Tuscans too, by a strange combination, but is so little known, owing to his scorn of the usual claptrap and catchpenny arts. Willard Fiske[7] our compatriot, a child of "Cornell," and supposed Icelandic scholar, who lives in Mr. Marsh's[8] old villa, and has filled it with 5000 volumes of the Sagas and of Petrarch (!!) is, though friendly and hospitable, an absolutely colourless little personage. The other Americans there are *nil*. (I am staying here— provisionally—with my old friend Mrs. Bronson (who lived, a thousand years ago, at Newport and has lived here for ten). Her house directly faces the big doors of the Salute Church—and is next to the Pension Suisse, where I think you once stayed. But I am lodged in an old palazzo Giustinian-Recanati, which, in her rear, forms a kind of detached wing or appendage to her premises. It contains a very snug and comfortable little apartment of several rooms, including a private theatre, very well mounted, which she most benevolently puts at the service of her friends. Browning[9] has often staid here—by the month at a time (he is a great friend of the padrona) and written crabbed verses at the table at which I sit. His son has been staying here for three months and departed just before I came in. They are looking for a palace—he and Robert—want to *buy* one—and thought they had, last year, till the vendor backed out. Mr. "Peabody Russell"[10] of the U.S. has just bought two Contarini palaces, and is going to "knock them into one"! I tremble for what that one will be. This visit of mine (to Mrs. B.) has been promised again and again—but I shall make it short and soon look out for an independent lodging. Mrs. Bronson is a most benevolent, injudiciously (even) generous woman, adored by all the common people of Venice—and preyed upon by her servants. "Society" here presses more or less into her saloons—Layards, Hurtados, Mocenigos, Metternichs, Don Carlos (!!)[11] etc.—but I have kept out of them, mostly, save when she is alone (with her only daughter, a plain but pleasant girl, whose hand is sought here by penniless patricians who think her richer than she is, and whom she doesn't at all fancy. She doesn't like Venice—and would fain live in England.) I am overdone with *people* and aspire to

be quiet here, and do my work and possess my soul.—
Yes, London is a *man*'s city (not a woman's)—but even
a man may sometimes be glad of something smaller.
I am happy to say, however, that I always remain of
the mind that if one can only have—or if *I* can only
have—one domicile, London is the best place to have
it. There it covers most ground. England is interesting
at present—because it is heaving so, and cracking and
fermenting. But the fissures are mainly political, and
the exhalations often foul. Besides, I miss there the
literary sense. *Il n'y en a plus!*—nor anywhere else, that I
can see. I shall be delighted to see Lowell and Lily—so
that I talk with her—and with him—about you. I envy
you immensely your long reads; that is the curse of
London—it is the worst place in the world for reading.
Ever my dear Grace, your affectionate

Henry James

NOTES

1. Grace Norton (1834–1926), the sister of Charles Eliot Norton (1827–1908), the Harvard art historian, translator of Dante and the founder of *The Nation*.

2. Alice James (1848–1892), sister of William and Henry, invalid since her father's death; she was the author of a *Diary* which was published only in 1964 by Leon Edel. She arrived in England in 1884: from her invalid room she kept in touch with the world.

3. Constance Fenimore Woolson (1840–1894), the American writer, a close friend of James. She committed suicide in Venice (see Introduction).

4. Violet Paget (Vernon Lee) (1856–1935), the English writer who lived in Florence. Her brother Eugene Lee Hamilton (1845–1907) told the anecdote that gave James the idea for *The Aspern Papers (Letters*, III, p.167). As is well known, James transferred the story of the precious letters from Florence to Venice.

5. Teresa Guiccioli Gamba, the famous last mistress of Lord Byron.

6. Adolf von Hildebrand (1847–1921), a German sculptor who lived between Florence and Munich.

7. Willard Fiske (1831–1904), a scholar of the literature of Iceland, where he sojourned and kept a notebook of his 1879 stay; of Petrarch and Dante, of the Egyptian alphabet, and of the game of chess (he was editor of the American *Chess Monthly* in 1857, and in 1858–60 with P. Morphy). He left his Icelandic literature and his Dante collections to Cornell University; in the 1880s he printed several books in Florence. Cornell

University Press published several catalogues of the collections he bequeathed to the Library.

8. George Perkins Marsh (1800–1882), minister to Italy 1861–1862.

9. Robert Browning, who died in Venice in 1889. His son "Pen", married a rich American, Fannie Coddington, bought the huge Palazzo Rezzonico in 1889. His previous arrangements made with Count Montecuccoli ("the vendor") to buy from him the Palazzo Contarini dal Zaffo failed.

10. Mr. Peabody Russell bought both Palazzo Contarini Corfù and Palazzo Contarini dagli Scrigni, on the Grand Canal.

11. Sir Henry Layard (1817–1894), the diplomat and discoverer of Niniveh, lived with his wife Enid in Palazzo Cappello, on the Grand Canal, between Rialto and the Academy. Also Prince Paul Metternich (1834–1906), with his wife Mélanie, lived in Venice, and so did Don Carlos of Bourbon (1848–1909), from 1876. Don Carlos, duke of Madrid and the pretender to the throne of Spain, lived in Palazzo Loredan, at San Vio. The Mocenigos were an ancient patrician family of Venice.

IV

To Sarah Butler Wister[1]
February 27*th* [1887]   Venice, Palazzino Alvisi
(Edel III)   Canal Grande

Dear Mrs. Wister.

It would be a history to tell you why I have waited
till this hour—and till I should be in this place—to
answer your valued letter of so many weeks ago. To
put that history in three words—I have been, from the
moment it came—or from a certain time afterward—
been expecting, from one week to the other, to go to
Rome, and I wanted to give myself—and you!—the
satisfaction (in the hour I should spend with you) of
the Roman medium. Never, never have I forgotten
how some of the most ineffaceable impressions
of my life were gathered there fifteen years ago, in
your society. But month has followed month—and I
haven't yet gone to Rome—and, strange as it may
appear to you, it seems a little doubtful that I shall
manage it. Therefore you must have your letter now
and here. I came to Italy on December 1st; and have
spent in Florence the whole time that has elapsed
since then—until five days ago. My winter has taken
a different turn from my first plan.—I am staying
abroad twice as long, and dividing my time between
Florence and Venice. I was to have gone to Rome on

February 1st—but it proved just the thing, when the moment came, that I didn't want to do—owing to the shoals *of people* with whom my visit would have been associated. I came abroad to escape 'em (the human race—excuse my fastidiousness!) but I found myself much mixed up with them in Florence—so that it was more difficult than I had hoped to get time for reading (for which there is horribly little time in London—so that I depend on my foreign excursions to make it up) and generally possessing my soul. But behold, every one I had ever heard of, and I didn't want to hear of again, was ascertained by me to be either in Rome or on the way there—so that I foresaw the shipwreck of all my hopes of concentration. I foresaw that inevitably my life would intertwine with a thousand irrelevancies. In a word, it was plain that I wouldn't be unknowing and unknown (excuse my fatuity!) so that I put it off. This was the easier to do as one's stomach is really turned here by the accounts of the hideous things that are being wrought upon the helpless seven hills. Destruction and vulgarization everywhere—and the Villa Ludovisi cut up into building lots. The Villa Ludovisi—*-je ne vous dis que cela*! I staid in Florence till February 22nd and then came here for an indefinite number of weeks. I find it delightfully quiet—though I am staying—for the moment—with the good Mrs. Bronson. She has a little apartment—a sort of detached wing or pavilion, in the rear of her house—which she kindly puts at the disposition of her friends.

I occupy it—in pursuance of a frequent promise—for the present, but shall seek an independent lodging as soon as I civilly may. Venice is wintry yet and so little *terne*, in consequence; also the *calles* and *campos* impress the sense with a kind of glutinous, malodorous damp. But it is Venice, none the less, and it is a ravishment to be here and to think that every week, at this season, will bring out a little more of the colour. I have a hope, if I stay in Italy late enough, of going down to Rome for ten days in May—when the damaging crowd shall have taken itself off. I dream then of also taking a little tour of old towns in Tuscany. If I am able to do this I shall certainly give you news of Rome [. . .]

February 28th. I had to break off my letter yesterday, and since then we have been a good deal flurried by further personal accounts of the wretched contagious scare produced on the Riviera by the recent earthquake-shocks, of which the full report will have come to you in the U.S.—that is, I saw last evening the Daniel Curtises,[2] of Boston (she, you may remember, a sister of that melancholy and strenuous, but estimable and superior, Miss Wormeley[3] of Newport, who has lately been so incongruously—as a New England old-maid, unacquainted with French—and other badnesses—

mistranslating Balzac); which D. Curtises have just fled back from the frightened though not hurt Monte Carlo—to the splendid Palazzo Barbaro, of which they are the enviable owners (they have bought it) here. The Riviera has been full of people we know—and many, no doubt (lots of Bostonians) known to you; and the sudden violent, alarmed break-up and stampede of the luxurious colony (though unaccompanied by any real injury—except to the poor people who live by its presence there)—have been really melancholy and sickening. I hear of Mrs. Mason and her Balfours, passing their nights in a *carriage* at Monte Carlo—where they have had a villa.

March 1st. I was again interrupted—yesterday—but this time I vow I shall have my talk with you out. The day is lovely—and the golden glow of Venice streams into my room. On laying down my pen yesterday I went out and in the course of the afternoon paid a visit to a most remarkable woman—the Countess Pisani[4]—a lady who vaguely suggests Caterina Cornaro and makes one believe in the romantic heroines of D'Israeli and Bulwer.[5] She has English blood in her veins—her father was the doctor who bled Byron to death at Missolonghi—and her mother a French odalisque out of the harem of the Grand Turk. The late Count Pisani married her thirty-five years ago for her beauty which must have been extraordinary and still is very striking (she is fifty-five and looks about forty); she has spent all her life in Italy; and today widowed, childless, palaced, villaed, pictured, jewelled, and modified by Venetian society in a kind of mysterious awe—she passes for a great personage and the biggest swell—on the whole—in the place. She is very little in Venice—living mainly at her villa on the mainland, where she farms a large property with un-Venetian energy. She made an impression—on me—as of one not formed of the usual social stuff of today—but the sort of woman one might have found—receiving on a balcony, here—at 2 o'clock on a June morning—in the early years of the century [. . .] I am ever your affectionate old friend

Henry James

NOTES

1. Sarah Butler Wister (1835–1908), the daughter of the famous actress Fanny Kemble.

2. Daniel Sargent Curtis (1825–1908) and his wife Ariana Wormeley Curtis (1833–1922) had established themselves in Venice, becoming the owners of Palazzo Barbaro in 1885. They had two children, Osborne (1858–1918) and Ralph (1854–1922), the latter a painter and a friend of Sargent, whose cousin he was on his mother's side.

3. Katherine Prescott Wormeley (1830–1908), the sister of Ariana Wormeley Curtis and the translator of Balzac, Bourget, Dumas, St. Beuve.

4. Evelin van Millingen (1830–1902) married the last of the Pisani of Santo Stefano, Almorò. Her mother, a French woman, had not come "out of the harem of the grand Turk", but, having lived in Constantinople for thirty years, she had written an autobiographical volume, *Thirty Years in a Harem*, having had as her second husband the Turkish ambassador H. H. Kibrizli-Mehemet Pasha. Caterina Cornaro was Queen of Cyprus in the fifteenth century and on the death of her husband James II she left her reign to the Republic of Venice, retiring to Asolo where she held court. See F. Colasanti, *Dizionario Biografico degli Italiani.*, vol. 22, Rome, 1979. Caterina Cornaro was quite a legendary figure in the XIX century. (Ariana Curtis's cat was called Caterina Cornaro).

5. Benjamin Disraeli (1804–1881) and Bulwer-Lytton (1803–1873), at the time very well known as novelists.

V

To Francis Boott[1]
March 15*th* [1887]   Palazzino Alvisi
(Edel III)   Canal Grande

My dear Francis.

I am much gratified by your letter, which renews
the chain of intercourse. It comes to me on a dark
dripping un-Venetian morning which is the third or
fourth of a dismal series. Yesterday there were sinister
carts in the Piazza and men who looked like Irishmen
shovelling away snow. One was almost sorry to have
left Boston. Can one indeed say one has, with Daniel
Curtis, here, doing his best (though he abuses "over
there" so much) to make the Grand Canal seem
like Beacon Street,[2] I see them pretty often and they
are very friendly. But one calculates the time when
one shall have worked through his anecdotes and
come out the other side. Perhaps one never does—
it is an unboreable—or unbearable—St. Gothard.
I have gone several times to see Laura—Wagnière-
Huntington—[3] and Mabel—and find the latter indeed,
as you say, made of heroic stuff; to the impression of
which her Medea-beauty greatly adds. Her situation
is terribly touching—and you can form no idea,
until you have heard it from their own lips and also
those of the Curtises, of the *horrors* of that combined

tragedy of the earthquake and Henry H[untington]'s unmanageable madness. The helplessness of the two women (after the Curtises left them) and the details of the whole thing were too miserable [. . .] The quiet of this place is comfortable to me after the lively bustle of Florence. There are tea-parties here but one doesn't hear the clatter of the cups. I am accepting for the time the hospitality of this little palazzo Giustinian-Recanati in Mrs. Bronson's rear; but I have my own ménage, and reserve, pretty well, my freedom. Your Florentine Mr. B[rowning] is here—for a week, but is dimmed by a cold. I think I can never have written "very pleased" except dramatically—in the mouth of someone speaking—*è vero*? It is, however, very possible that I may have written very possible in *propria persona*. Tell Fenimore I forgive her—but only an angel would. She will understand. Much love to Lizzie and *tanti saluti* to the two gentlemen. Ever yours faithfully

Henry James

NOTES

1. Francis Boott (1813–1904), the American musician and composer, with his daughter Lizzie (1846–1888), who married the painter Frank Duveneck (1848–1919) and died young, from 1848 lived in Italy, after the death of his wife and child. He went back to the U.S. after the death of Lizzie, in 1889.

2. The famous Boston Street.

3. Laura Huntington Wagnière, American, the niece of sculptor Horatio Greenough, married the Swiss-Italian banker Henry Wagnière (Edel, *Letters* III, p.226).

VI

To Mrs. Daniel S. Curtis
April 23*rd* [1887]   Villa Bricchieri
(Edel III)   Bellosguardo

Dear Mrs. Curtis.

I send you this by the hand of my valued friend M. Paul
Bourget,[1] who will already have been very considerably
introduced to you. He goes to Venice for a month; I
take the greatest interest in him, and I can give him no
better proof of it than to put it in his power to know Mr.
Curtis and you. You will also not consider that I have
been moved by anything less than extreme sympathy
in making you acquainted with so agreeable and
distinguished a person. Please let him see the flicker of
the canal on your gilded roof—and take him over to
the garden and show him the garden-house. I envy him,
at the mere thought! I hoped to have been in Venice
during his stay—and then I should have brought him to
you. But I shall assist in spirit at your *causeries* and bless
your relations. Believe me, in advance, very gratefully
yours, and Mr. Curtis's—

Henry James

NOTE

1. Paul Bourget (1852–1935), the French writer, whose novel
Cosmopolis portrays the cosmopolitan expatriate society of Italy.

VII

To Catherine Walsh[1]
June 16*th* [1887]   Venice: (Palazzo Barbaro)
(Edel III)

Dearest Aunt.

As usual, when I am just on the point of writing to you comes in a good letter from you: with the date of May 30th [. . .] I am in Venice as you see—for the second time since I have come abroad. My stay, which will have been of a month this time, draws to a close—I depart on the 25th. It is piping hot but as beautiful as ever. I have been paying a long visit—long for me, who like less and less as I grow older, to stay with people, to the Daniel Curtises, formerly of Boston but who have been living here for years and are the owners of this magnificent old palace—all marble and frescoes and portraits of Doges—a delightful habitation for hot weather. Mrs. Curtis is a sister of Miss Wormeley of Newport, whom she much resembles in face— and she and her husband are very intelligent, clever and hospitable people. I came for ten days, and they have simply kept me on. Dick Walsh came to see me a couple of days ago—and yesterday I took him over to the Lido. He seems a very good and gentlemanly little fellow—but without much "culture" or general information—though fond of art and artists. Mrs.

Curtis has invited him to a party here, tonight. He is much with the McClellans,[2] the General's widow, son and daughter—and very devoted to the latter, a rather flippant spoiled girl, who has got into a peck of trouble here by writing a strangely indiscreet and reprehensible letter to the New York *World* about Venetian "society," which received her very well last winter. The strange things of that sort that the American female does!—as witness the terrible Mrs. Sherwood, poor "Posy" Emmet's mother-in-law. She invited me (and some others) to dine with her in London last summer, and then wrote a fearful letter about it (I having gone, all unconscious) to the American journals, which she afterwards sent me as if I should be delighted to see it [. . .] I will write again as soon as I get back to London, and am meanwhile ever your loving nevvy

Henry James

NOTES

1. Catherine Walsh (aunt Kate), the sister of Henry's mother. She died in 1899.

2. The McClellans: General George B. McClellan's (1826–1885) widow and children. He had been the General commanding northern forces during the Civil War, and was defeated by Abraham Lincoln in the 1864 presidential campaign.

VIII

To Thomas Bailey Aldrich[1]
June 21*st* [1887]   Venice.
(Edel III)

My dear Aldrich.

I send you today the remainder and end of "The
Aspern Papers"—the Tale in two parts of which I
sent you the First and a portion of the Second Part
about ten days ago (on the 12th ult.). I wrote to you
at some length about the story on that occasion—so
that there is nothing now to add save the hope the
accompanying may quickly and safely rejoin its pre-
decessor. Ever yours

Henry James

NOTE

1. Thomas Bailey Aldrich (1836–1907), a writer and the
director of the *Atlantic Monthly* from 1881 to 1890; he lived in
Boston from 1865. In March-May 1888 he published *The Aspern
Papers* in the journal (Edel, *Letters* III, p.186).

IX

To Grace Norton
July 23*rd*, 1887   34 De Vere Gardens W.
(Edel III)

My dear Grace.

I am ashamed to find myself back in England without
having fulfilled the inward vow I took when I received
your last good and generous letter—that of writing to
you before my long stay on the continent was over. But
I *almost* don't fail of that vow—inasmuch as I returned
only day before yesterday. My eight months' escape
into the happy immunities of foreign life is over and
the stern realities of London surround me; in the shape
of stuffy midsummer heat (that of this metropolis has
a truly British ponderosity—it's as dull as an article
in a Quarterly), smoke, circulars, invitations, *bills*,
the one sauce that Talleyrand commemorated, and
reverberations of the grotesque Jubilee. On the other
hand my small home seems most pleasant and peculiar
(in the sense of being my own), and my servants are
as punctual as they are prim—which is saying much.
But I enjoyed my absence, and I shall endeavour to
repeat it every year, for the future, on a smaller scale:
that is, to leave London, not at the beginning of the
winter but at the end, by the mid-April, and take the
period of the insufferable Season regularly in Italy.

It was a great satisfaction to me to find that I am as fond of that dear country as I ever was—and that its infinite charm and interest are one of the things in life to be most relied upon. I was afraid that the dryness of age—which drains us of so many sentiments—had reduced my old *tendresse* to a mere memory. But no—it is really so much in my pocket, as it were, to feel that Italy is always there. It is rather rude, my dear Grace, to say all this to you—for whom it is there to so little purpose. But if I should observe this scruple about all the places that you don't go to, or are not in, when I write to you, my writing would go very much on one leg. I was back again in Venice—where I paid a second visit late in the season (from the middle of May to July 1st)—when I got your last letter. I was staying at the Palazzo Barbaro, with the Daniel Curtises—the happy owners, today, of that magnificent house—a place of which the full charm only sinks into your spirit as you go on living there, seeing it in all its hours and phases. I went for ten days, and they clinging to me, I staid five weeks: the longest visit I ever paid a "private family." The Curtises are very private—and a most singular, original and entertaining couple. If I were lolling in one of your arm-chairs I could tell you more—but I can't describe them as I scribble here without the disloyalty of *incompleteness*—so it is better to reserve them for the great occasion of the future, whenever it may come, when I shall *talk* everything my pen hasn't been able to manage. They were most friendly and hospitable—but I don't *think* I shall stay with them again—if I can avoid it without rudeness. They can't keep their hands off their native land, which they loathe—and their perpetual digs at it fanned (if a dig can fan), my patriotism to a fever. In the interval between my two visits to Venice I took again some rooms at the Villa Brichieri at Bellosguardo—the one just below your old Ombrellino—where I had stayed for three December weeks on my arrival in Florence [. . .] I think of you on your porch—amid all your creepers and tendrils; and wherever you are, dear Grace, I am your very faithful and much remembering friend,

Henry James

X

To Isabella Stewart Gardner
May 15*th* [1890]   Milan[1], H. de la Ville
(I.S.G.M. Ms.)

Dear Mrs. Gardner.

Your truly attractive note which overtakes me at this
place this morning, exercises its attraction unimpaired
over channels and alps. I left London but three days
ago, with unconscious and (to myself, injurious)
perversity, at the very moment you were reaching it.
But of course you are coming down here. By "down
here" I mean to the sweetest land on earth—I care
not with which you compare it. Don't waste time—
and your figure—on Mr. Worth[2] and Paris, but come
and feel with me—somehow and somewhere—the
truth of the axiom just enunciated—Let your figure
be reflected in the clear lagoon, say, sometime after
June 1st. It will meet mine in the same soft element
and perhaps condescend to be occasionally seen in
juxtaposition with it. Before June 1st I move about—
going to as many little brown cities as I can: but for
June I hope to float. Therefore come, if you won't
sink me. At any rate I hope very much you'll be in
England the last half of the summer—for I return
the 1st days of August, when the London season is
over.

Ever faithfully yours

Henry James

De Vere Gardens always follows me.

NOTES

1. The letterhead is "34, De Vere Gardens", and this explains the post scriptum.

2. The famous Parisian couturier.

XI

To Alice James
June 6*th* [1890]   [Venice], Palazzo Barbaro
(Edel III)

Dearest Sister,

I am ravished by your letter after reading the play[1]
(keep it locked up, safe and secret, though there are
three or four copies in existence) which quite makes
me feel as if there had been a triumphant première
and I had received overtures from every managerial
quarter and had only to count my gold [. . .] You
might hint to W[illiam] that you have read the piece
under seal of secrecy to me and think so-and-so of
it—but are so bound (to me) not to give a sign that *he*
must bury what you tell him in tenfold mystery. But I
doubt if even *this* would be secure—it would be in the
Transcript the next week—Venice continues adorable
and the Curtises the soul of benevolence. Their
upstairs apartment (empty and still unoffered—at
forty pounds a year—to any one but me) beckons me
so, as a foot-in-the-water here, that if my dramatic
ship had begun to come in, I should probably be
tempted to take it at a venture—for all it would
matter. But for the present I resist perfectly—
especially as Venice isn't *all* advantageous. The great
charm of such an idea is the having in Italy, a little

cheap and private refuge independent of hotels etc., which every year grow more disagreeable and German and tiresome to face—not to say dearer too. But it won't be for this year—and the Curtises won't let it. What Pen Browning has done here, through his American wife's dollars, with the splendid Palazzo Rezzonico, transcends description for the beauty, and, as Ruskin would say, "wisdom and Tightness" of it. It is altogether royal and imperial—but "Pen" isn't kingly and the *train de vie* remains to be seen. Gondoliers ushering in friends from pensions won't fill it out. The Rodgerses[2] have turned up but are not oppressive—seeming mainly to be occupied with being constantly ill. That is Katie appears everywhere to collapse badly and expensively, and I judge she has something grave the matter with her. She has "doctors" at every place they go—is in bed for days etc.—and yet they go everywhere. I don't encourage them (I have indeed seen them but once—when I took them on the water by moonlight), to talk about "the will"—as it's disagreeable and they really know nothing about it. I am thinking, after all, of joining the Curtises in the evidently most beautiful *drive* (of upwards of a week, with rests), they are starting upon on the 14th, from a place called Vittorio[3], in the Venetian Alps, two hours' rail from there, through Cadore, Titian's country, the Dolomites etc., toward

Oberammergau. They offer me, pressingly, the fourth seat in the carriage that awaits them when they leave the train—and also an extra ticket they have taken for the play at Oberammergau if I choose to go so far. This I shall scarcely do, but I *shall* probably leave with them, drive four or five days and come *back*, via Verona, by rail—leaving my luggage here. Continue to address here—unless, before that, I give you one other address while I am gone. I shall find all letters here, on my return, if I do go, in the keeping of the excellent *maestro di casa*—the Venetian Smith. I should be back, at the *latest*, by the 25th—probably by the 20th. In this case I shall presumably go back to Florence to spend four or five days with Baldwin[4] (going to Siena or Perugia); after which I have a dream of going up to Vallombrosa (nearly 4000 feet above the sea—but of a softness!) for two or three weeks— till I have to leave Italy on my way home. I am writing to Edith Peruzzi[5] who has got a summer-lodge there, and is already there, for information about the inn. If I don't go there I shall perhaps try Camaldoli or San Marcello—all high in the violet Appennines, within three or four hours; and mainly by a little carriage, of Florence. But I *want* to compass Vallombrosa, which I have never seen and have always dreamed of and which I am assured is divine—infinitely salubrious and softly cool. The idea of lingering in Italy a few

weeks longer on these terms is very delightful to me—
it does me, as yet, nothing but good. But I shall see.
I put B.'s letter in another envelope. I rejoice in your
eight gallops—they may be the dozen now.
Ever your

Henry

NOTES

1. The play from *The American*, staged in London on September
26, 1891, was not a success. From 1890 to 1994 James wrote for
the theatre.

2. Relatives on Henry's mother's side (Edel, *Letters* III, p.289).

3. Vittorio Veneto, the former Ceneda. Titian's country is
Cadore, and more specifically Pieve di Cadore where he was
born.

4. William Wilberforce Baldwin (1850–1910), an American
doctor living in Florence. James's letters to him are full of
sympathy for the doctor's own children.

5. Edith Story, the daughter of the sculptor and writer William
Wetmore Story (1819–1895), permanently a resident of Italy
from 1851. She married the Florentine marquis Ubaldo Peruzzi.

XII

To Isabella Stewart Gardner
June 24*th* 1890   Garmisch, Bavaria
(Edel III)

Dear Mrs. Gardner.

There are many things I must ask you to excuse. One
of them is this paper from the village grocer of an
unsophisticated Bavarian valley. The others I will
tell you when we next meet. Not that they matter
much; for you *won't* excuse them—you never do.
But I have your commands to write and tell you "all
about" something or other—I think it was Venice—
and at any rate Venice will do. Venice always does.
Therefore I won't give you further grounds for rigour
by failing to obey your behest on this point. I have
just been (three days ago) to see the Passion Play
at Oberammergau, and with my good friends and
hosts the Curtises, with whom, twelve days ago, I
left Venice to drive hither, delightfully, through the
Venetian Alps, the Dolomites, Cadore, Cortina, the
Ampezzo etc., I am resting, after that exploit, in
this sweet recess among the mountains—which has
been (it is but two hours away by carriage) our *point
de départ* for the pilgrimage. Tomorrow we drive back
to Innsbruck and separate—they to go to England
and I back to Italy, for two or three weeks more. The

Passion Play is curious, tedious, touching, intensely respectable and intensely German. I wouldn't have come if I hadn't been brought (by Mrs. Curtis and Miss Wormeley); and I shall never go again even if I *am* brought by syren hands. But all these Tyrolean countries are beyond praise—and the several days' drive was magnificent. Venice was cool, empty, melancholy and delicious. They "sprang" upon me (the Curtises) the revelation that you are to have the Barbaro for August, torturing me thus with a vision of alternatives and preferences—the question of whether I would give up the happy actual (the secure fact of really *being* there in June) for the idea of a perhaps even happier possible or impossible, the romance of being there in August. I took what I had—I *was* there—a fortnight. Now I am going back, to stay but a day or two, and then do some other things—go again for ten days to Florence and to two or three Tuscan excursions. Why are you so perverse?—Why do you come to London when I am away, and away from it just when I come back? Even your bright presence there does not make me repent having fled this year from the Savage Season. You wouldn't have made it tame—so what good should I have got? I hope you have found it as wild as you like things. The Palazzo Barbaro is divine, and divinely still: don't make it spin round. If I am in Italy still when you arrive *je viendrai vous y voir.* But I take it you have arranged your court. My clothes are there still (I only brought a necktie here). But I shall get them out of your way—you would perhaps pitch them into the Adriatic. I shall write to you again and am ever, dear Mrs. Gardner, most faithfully yours

Henry James

XIII

To Grace Norton
June 30*th* [1890]   Venice, Palazzo Barbaro
(Edel III)

My dear Grace.

I begin this grateful letter to you with vague ideas as to when I shall finish it—being at the present moment on a branch that sways beneath me: i.e. in Venice only for twenty-four hours, *di passaggio*, on my way to other parts. But the great thing *is* to begin—for after all I should never properly and justifiably end—telling you how I glow with genial appreciation of the two magnanimous letters I have received from you since I came to Italy, and more particularly with gratitude for the second one, on the subject of my latest "work" (date of June 12th), which I found here last evening on my return from an excursion (mainly driving), of fifteen days through the Dolomites and to the Oberammergau Passion Play. I came hither originally June 1st, to spend a fortnight with my old friends and entertainers the D-[1] (*you* will say the d—d) Curtises, according to a promise made and renewed any time these three years. This promise I redeemed, very agreeably (to myself), and then unexpectedly started off with my hosts, who had made their plans—and *mine* (which I hadn't) to proceed by carriage through the

110

Venetian Alps, Cadore, Cortina, the Ampezzo, etc., to (by the aid of five further hours of rail) Innsbruck, and thence by carriage (forty miles) through the Bavarian Highlands and the pastoral valley of Garmisch, to the before-mentioned inevitable Ammergau—which is the "boom" this summer and every tenth year. To make a long story short, I started with them, to see Cadore etc., and then was wooed on by adorable scenery, genial society and lovely weather to do, from day to day, the whole thing—which I have gratefully survived but not allowed to cheat me out of a return to Italy, where I hope to remain till August 1st. I posted back to Innsbruck with my friends (after the curious, tedious, touching Ammergau episode—very honourable on the part of the earnest and practical peasants and artisans who act the play, but well nigh threatened with extinction by vulgarity and cocknification from Cook, Gaze, etc.—the entrepreneurs of British and American travel); and there we separated, the kind Curtises to betake themselves to England to see their younger son who dwells there in country-gentlemanliness (at least attempted), and matrimony, and I to come back and pick up my luggage and clothing—represented during our drive only by an exiguous wallet. I go with them tomorrow to Florence—and meanwhile I am spending this splendid summer day in this beautiful empty house, under the care of the suavest and most obsequious of old Venetian butlers. Such is a succinct account of my recent doings—to which let me add, that I go to Florence, first to stay four or five days with a good friend I have there—a dear little American physician of genius, W.W. Baldwin by name; who makes the rain and the fine weather there now; and then to go up (if I can find a perch at the inn) and spend the rest of July on the divine hilltop of Vallombrosa—which is high enough to be cool and lovely enough to be warm. After that, my holiday finished, I shall post back to London, where work awaits me and where I shall not scruple to spend, most contentedly and unfashionably, the rest of the summer.

July 3rd (three days later): Via Palestro, Firenze. I take up my little story again here—having been interrupted just after those last words and transferred myself day before yesterday from Venice to this place. This is a delightful moment to be in Italy, and really nowadays, the only right one—for the herd of tourists has departed, the scramble at the stations is no more, and one seems alone with the dear old land, who at the same time, seems alone with herself. I am happy to say that I am as fond as ever of this tender little Florence, where it doesn't seem a false note even to be staying with an "American doctor." My friend Baldwin is a charming and glowing little man, who, coming here eight or ten years ago, has made himself a first place, and who seems to consider it a blessing to him that I should abide a few days in his house. I accept the oddity of the view, and perhaps even regard it as another oddity, all round, that on leaving him, I shall probably go up and spend a week with the Edith Peruzzis, *née* Story, at Vallombrosa. As to this I am temporizing—but I am distinctly *pressed*; or should say I was if my modesty permitted me to. I should have liked to tell you how fascinating I found the Italian Alps and the Tyrol—what a "revelation" they really struck me as being—revelation, I mean, of the sympathetic, and loveable in great mountain scenery. I never "sympathised" much with Switzerland—but I can with the Dolomites. When, three mornings ago, I rose early, to take the train for Florence, and in the cool, fresh 7 o'clock light, was rowed through the delicious half-stirred place and the imbroglio of little silent plashing waterways to the station, it was really heartbreaking to come away—to come out into the dust and *banalité* of the rest of the world. (Venice clings closer to one by its dustlessness than perhaps by any other one charm.) But already the sweetness of Florence *tastes.* I am, however, seriously thinking, or rather *dreaming*, of putting my hand on some little cheap permanent refuge in Venice—some little perch over the water, with a bed and a table in it, to call one's own and come away to, without the interposition of luggage and hotels, whenever the weight of London, at certain times, is no longer to be borne. For the moment, however, I am just solicited back there by a local (or would be) Lorelei in the shape of Mrs. Jack Gardner, whom the absent Curtises have lent Palazzo Barbara to for the month of August and who requests the favour of my company (she seems to think I am "thrown in") after the second or third. I have left to the end, my dear Grace, thanking you properly for the very "handsome" way in which you speak of the massive *[Tragic] Muse*. I am delighted that it strikes you as a success, for I tried so hard to make it one that if it hadn't been it would have been a failure indeed. That's all I can say about it—as I never have begun to understand how one can "justify" a work of art or imagination or *take up* anything said on the subject. One's own saying is what one has tried to say in it. This is there or it's absent, and when the thing is done nothing will make it better or worse. Thank you for reading. Good-bye: I wish you had a little change as they say in London.

May this bring you a moment of such.

Ever faithfully yours

Henry James

NOTE

1. D for Daniel (Curtis).

XIV

To Ariana Curtis
July 7*th* [1890]
(Dartmouth Ms.)

Florence, Villino Rubio
1 Via Palestro

Dear Mrs. Curtis

I have delayed too long to write to you—but this has been not from any slackness of impulse, but from a sort of sense that I ought to have remarkable adventures to relate (to justify, in your eyes, my romantic return to Italy), whereas my adventures have been, in fact, though very pleasant, not in the least a challenge to admiration. It is, however, useless, to wait longer for the wonderful. I spent yesterday at Vallombrosa and I go this afternoon to Siena for three days—but everything happened, and doubtless will happen (*absit omen!*) in the most normal conditions. Quite the most thrilling of my experiences since we parted was to go back to the beautiful empty Barbaro and spend 36 hours there with a grand usurped sense of its being my own. For this is what I had the arrogance to do—I ought long since to have notified you of it. I arrived at 6 o'clock, with the intention of simply picking up my clothes and sleeping that night. But the next a.m. it was not in human nature to tear itself away! The day was delicious, Angelo and Elisa[1] were even more so and your marble halls suffused with the "tender" note of

115

your absence were most pleading and irresistible of all.
I strutted about in them with a successful effort of self-
deception and tasted for once the feelings of earthly
greatness. To say that Angelo was hospitable and that
the Tita waited upon me both on my arrival and on
my departure, is but faintly to sketch the situation. I
spent a good bit of the day with Mrs. Bronson, whom
I caught just as she was starting for Greifenberg in
Styria—of course with a Montalba.[2] They have gone
for bronchial waters and come back on the 20th. This
she had revealed to me in advance by telegraph—
so that Asolo had to drop out of my programme. I
gave up the drive over the mountains thitherward in
consequence, and did the whole thing from Innsbruck
to Venice by rail—stopping however a day at Trent
and a couple of days at Verona. Trent was somehow
disappointing and drenched, absolutely reeking, with
the electric light. *En revanche* there was no water—that
is there was none at the hotel and I couldn't have a
bath! Surely Trent *ought* to become Italian. At Verona
I collapsed upon my old hotel—which, however, this
time I found excellent and not exceptionally dear.
It was very hot, and the Colombo d'Oro is *not* on a
square, but in a back street (*near* the Arena) and I found
it. Edith Bronson was soon to start for Zoldo with the
Edens,[3] and her mother expects to join them, I believe,
on her return from Greifenberg. I spent an hour at

the Edens' garden (whence I took Mme Wiel[4] home in a sociable sandolo (or sand*rolo*?)[5] and the question was there broached of *my* also joining them about August 1st. But I see little chance of that—in spite of Mrs. Jack[6] having bespoken my company in your misappropriated (or at least disappropriated) home for any date that may suit me after the said 1st—an early date preferred. (I heard from her on this subject a week ago, but have not yet answered her.) This summer aspect of Italy is delightful to me; but my holiday is taking strides to its close—and my present prevision is that on August 1st I shall be jogging back to Reality over the Saint-Gothard. I have been in Florence for six days—where, even after 24 hours, the ache of quitting Venice that early morning, in the fresh, cool light, and being floated with such a heartbreaking, remonstrating plash—of *your* oars—down to the station was somewhat healed and assuaged. For Florence is empty now, and lovely, and "tender" too—and the impression of it is infinitely sweet. But it's dusty—and Venice isn't. I have seen Mrs. Huntington,[7] who has been ill again and is on the point of departing, with Mme Wagnière, for Andorno, in the Piemontese Alps. On the 12th I start for a little tour in out of the way Tuscany (to three or four places, e.g. those I have never heard of—did you ever hear of the sovereign city of Torretta (the Towered,) with my friend Baldwin and an Italian friend of his who is both an impiegato in the Ferrovie[8] and a man of culture, having his esoteric Tuscany at his fingers' ends. He undertakes to give us, in 5 or 6 days, the inside views of ancient cities and wonderful corners untrodden by tourists and commemorated by Dante. We go to Volterra, Montepulciano and Chiusi, and I know not where else. The programme involves, I believe, a good bit of driving and an intimate acquaintance with railway connections. We are to see the Casentino and the Mugello—in short I quite thirst for it. But in the meanwhile I go, till the 12th, this afternoon, to Siena. I have, further, for the 17th a room (a rare prize) engaged at the divine Vallombrosa, where by rising at 5 (you go from here,) I got ever so many hours, yesterday, of a lovely day. It struck me as one of the loveliest spots on earth and as deliciously cool and salubrious. Unfortunately the "accommodation" is only limited, in quantity, though the small hotel, the only one, seemed excellent. Some day you might do worse than try it—the woods, the walks, the views, the excursions, the places to stroll in, and sit, and spend the day in the open air, all being, apparently, exquisite and extremely numerous. The only blot is that one has to make sure of quarters a long time in advance—unless one stays with Mme Peruzzi: a privilege that I am actually engaged in wriggling out of. But I am overwhelming you with egotism, and I only, or mainly, want news of your own late proceedings. If you kindly find time in the rush of London to write me a word (but *don't* try for that—wait till you get into the country,) please address it to 34 De Vere Gardens, W. I hope that, after that last rather heated scramble at the Innsbruck station, you plunged into serene contemplation and that everything has gone well with you to this moment. I hope you made all your connections—but formed no new ones! I parted from Miss Wormeley that same day—after lunch—with her companions still somewhat in the vague . . . But I hope all that soon became definite and happy and that I shall see her in London. I shall be very keen about you and Mr. Daniel there. Please give him my love and all good wishes. Ever dear Mrs. Curtis, very faithfully

Henry James

NOTES

1. Like Tita, the servants of the Curtises.

2. The four Montalba sisters, with their parents and a brother, lived at Palazzo Trevisan, on the Zattere, in Venice. They all received some award for their artistic merits. Henrietta (1856–1893) as a sculptor, Clara (1842–1929) as a painter: the latter is the author of the pretty drawings that illustrated Mrs. Bronson's essay, *Browning in Asolo*. Ellen made a lovely portrait of Mrs. Bronson (1892), which is kept at "La Mura", in Mrs. Bronson's heirs' house, and which is published by Edel and Meredith.

3. Frederic (1828–1916) and Caroline (1837–1928) Eden lived in Palazzo Barbarigo. Mr. Eden was an invalid. They also had a famous garden on the Giudecca, called "The Garden of Eden".

4. Alethea Wiel, the author of several books on Venice and the Veneto region, the sister of the Barons Wenlock and the wife of Taddeo Wiel (1849–1920), a writer and musicologist, who catalogued the musical funds of the Marciana Library.

5. James's first choice is the right word: the boat is called "sandolo".

6. Mrs. Jack, as Mrs. Isabella Stewart Gardner was called.

7. Mrs. Huntington, the mother of Laura Huntington Wagnière, died in Florence in 1893.

8. "An employee in the Railways".

XV

To Ariana Curtis
July 10*th* [1892]   Venice, Palazzo Barbaro
(Edel III)

Dear Mrs. Curtis.

J'y suis—would that I could add *j'y reste*!—till you return. Many thanks for your kind London note. I rejoice in everything that may be comfortable in your situation or interesting in your adventures. I came hither two days ago and Mrs. J.L.G.[1] has kindly put a bed for me in this divine old library[2]—where I am fain to pass the livelong day. Have you ever *lived* here?—if you haven't, if you haven't gazed upward from your couch, in the rosy dawn, or during the postprandial (that is after-luncheon) siesta, at the medallions and arabesques of the ceiling, permit me to tell you that you don't *know* the Barbaro. Let me add that I am not here in wantonness or disorder—but simply because the little lady's other boarders are located elsewhere. I am so far from complaining that I wish I could stay here forever. I don't—I go out with the little lady, and even with the boarders. It is scorching scirocco, but I don't much care; it is the essence of midsummer, but I buy five-franc alpaca jackets and feel so Venetian that you might almost own me. I believe I am to go to Asolo for a day or two next week—and I confess that I have a dread of exchanging this marble hall for the top of a stable. But there is a big lady as well as a little one in the case—and I must execute myself. They went (Mrs. Jack and her three friends and Mr. Jack) last night to a première at the Malibran—an opera[3] with libretto by Viel, who had sent boxes and other blandishments. They roasted, I believe, all the more that they frantically applauded[*]—while I met the wandering airs on the lagoon. Mrs. Bronson is at Asolo and I've not seen her; Edith is with the Edens and I have, thank heaven, no cousins at the pensions. So it is a rather simplified Venice—save always for the boarders. I believe we are going—or they are going— to Fusina[4] (by steamboat) this evening: the little lady is of an energy! She showed me yesterday, at Carrer's[5] her seven glorious chairs (the loveliest I ever saw); but they are not a symbol of her attitude—she never sits down. I hope you have seen Dorchester House[6]—it is, however, but a public imitation of this. Yet the pictures are wondrous and Mrs. Holford herself almost the best.—No, I haven't—thank heaven—a single political opinion, unless it be one to be glad I'm out of it—out of the sweetness and light of the elections, I mean. I stay here, alas, but from day to day; when I haven't a cousin in Venice I have a brother in Switzerland. But

---

[*] *Que faire in a sent box à moins que l'on n'applaud?*

oh, how I dream of coming back! Please tell the Paron[7] how I pity him for not being here, and remind him that pity is akin to love. Ever yours, dear Mrs. Curtis, with the same pity

Henry James

NOTES

1. Isabella Stewart Gardner had rented Palazzo Barbaro and Henry James was her guest there.

2. The library of the Palazzo Barbaro, on the top floor, decorated with XVIII century chinoiseries and beautiful medallions and paintings on the ceiling. The bed was canopied, with a mosquito net, as documented by the photograph in the Isabella Stewart Gardner Museum collections.

3. The opera *Maometto II* by the Venetian Maestro Lorenzi-Fabris, which had a great success at the Malibran theatre, according to the *Gazzetta di Venezia* of July 11,1892. The libretto was the work of Taddeo Wiel (see letter XIV, Footnote 4).

4. Fusina was the boat terminal on the main land, from which one travelled on by coach.

5. One of the many antique dealers of XIX century Venice. The chairs had been bought at an auction in Rome, and were coming from the Borghese collection.

6. Dorchester House, in London, built by Lewis Vulliany in 1851, after the Rome Farnesina. It was later destroyed.

7. "The Master" in Venetian dialect.

XVI

To Isabella Stewart Gardner
Friday July 29*th* [1892]   Hôtel Richemont
(Edel III)   Lausanne

Dear Donna Isabella.

I have waited to draw breath here before writing to
you and I arrived here only yesterday. Italy is already
a dream and Venice a superstition. The Barbaro is a
phantom and Donna Isabella herself but an exquisite
legend. You all melt away in this hard Swiss light.
But I have just bought a tinted (I believe they call it
a "smoked" pince-nez), and I am attempting to focus
you again. I carried my bleeding heart, last Sunday,
all the way to Turin, where I literally spent two days
(the Hôtel de l'Europe there is excellent,) and finished
the abominable article.[1] With that atrocity on my
conscience I deserved nothing better, doubtless, than
the melancholy Mont Cenis, which dragged me last
Wednesday, through torrid heats, straight out of
Paradise, fighting every inch of the way. Switzerland
is much hotter than Italy, and, for beauty, not to be
mentioned in the same cycle of time. It's a pleasantry
to say it has charm. I have been here (in this particular
desolation,) since yesterday noon, intently occupied in
realizing that I am an uncle.[2] It is very serious—but
I am fully taking it in. I don't see as yet, how long I

shall remain one—but sufficient unto the day are the nephews thereof. Mine, here, are domiciled with *pastori* in the neighboring valleys, but were let loose in honour of my arrival. They are charming and the little girl a *bellezza*. My brother and his wife send you the friendliest greetings and thank you for all you have done—and are doing—for me. My windows, from this high hillside, hang over the big lake and sweep it from one end to the other, but the view isn't comparable to that of the little canal end from the divine library of the Barbaro. I am utterly homesick for Venice. *Il n'y a que ça.*—Our smash on the way to the station is almost an agreeable recollection to me—simply for being so Venetian. Gardner will have told you all about it, but I hope there have been no tiresome sequels. I don't know, but I *think* it arose from a want of competence on the part of the fallible Domenico, who had the prow-oar. I shall be eager to hear from you some day *ce qui en suivit*. I am hungry for Venetian and Asolan gossip. I want to know everything you have *bought* these last days—even for yourself. Or has *everything* been for me? I pray this may catch you before you start for this cruel country. I enclose the introducing word for Lady Brooke,[3] to whom I am also writing. My station here is precarious, as my brother, I believe, thinks of going somewhere else—so I don't venture to ask you to write anywhere but to De Vere Gardens (34)—if you are so charitable

as to write—or if you ever *can* write again after the handkissing extraordinary that I ween the Barbaro will witness on Monday. Please give my friendliest remembrance to Gardner, whom I thank, afresh, for his company and protection last Sunday a.m.—how long ago and far-away it seems! If he hadn't been there to steady the boat Domenico would probably have sent me to the bottom. I am more and more determined, however, in spite of such perils, to secure a Venetian home. I largely depend upon you for it, and I am, dear, generous lady,
Your *devotissimo*

Henry James

NOTES

1. The essay "The Grand Canal", published in *Scribner's Magazine* (XII, November 1892), and then collected in *Italian Hours* (see Edel, *Letters* III, p.392).

2. James had left Venice to go to Switzerland to see his brother William, with his wife Alice and their four children. He stayed in Switzerland for about ten days, a little disappointed because William left for a hiking tour of the Engadine only two days after Henry's arrival, and without telling him. (Edel, *The Middle Years*, pp.327–328, *Letters* III, p.392).

3. Margaret Alice Lili (née de Windt) Brooke (1849–1936), Ranee of Sarawak. She married Charles Anthony Johnson-Brooke in 1869, when he had been a rajah for a year, succeeding his uncle Sir James Brooke.

XVII

To Ariana Curtis
August 16*th* [1892]   34 De Vere Gardens. W.
(Dartmouth Ms.)

Dear Mrs. Curtis

I am delighted to learn by your charming letter that
there is an early prospect of seeing you. I was on the
point of writing to you to express the hope that there
might be. I came home two days ago—and though I
left Venice, and Italy, only the first days of this month,
I am again fiercely pining for them, or, *à défaut* of that,
pining for the chance and the whomwithal to talk
about them! As I gather that your experience of the
Norfolk *moeurs* will have left you with a similar appetite
I promise myself much joy when we meet. I had only a
trifle of 17 days at the Barbaro, but never had Venice
intertwined itself so with my affections. I have marked
it for my own, and this last visit completely settled for
me the question of the real necessity of a little *permanent*
perch or asylum there. I came within an ace of taking
a very modest one the day before I left—just out the
Grand Canal but looking straight into it—a house
that faces the side of Palazzo Foscari.[1] But I hadn't
time to complete the transaction, and it will be for my
next visit, which I shall make as soon as I can possibly
manage it. Mrs. Jack the wonderful has meanwhile a

commission to look out for me. She remained, to the end of my visit, the kindest and easiest of hostesses and the Barbaro the loveablest place in all the weary world. Your library (I mean the upstair one,) is a paradise of a bedroom—if you keep your stockings together. Such *dear* Summer-mornings as I had there! Angelo and Tita ministered with unfailing grace to one's faintest stirrings of wants. I don't wonder English country-society manners strike you as stiff. Heavens how I agree with you about the dull density of it all! But you have been spoiled—you have lived too much in Arcadia. I will tell you all the gossip of the Canal side; especially the wondrous Mrs. Bronson-Pen Browning tension and rift and make-up (over the Asolo houses). I went to Asolo, with Mrs. Jack, and *adored* it. I adored and adore everything in those parts. I missed Ralph at Ouchy, to my regret—and dodged the Blumenthals— to my relief. I too, however, did grandfather to my nephews and niece. Won't you kindly let me know the first moment you are "due"? I am impatient for you both, of both your *devotissimo*

Henry James

NOTE

1. Most likely this was the building where there is now the Masieri Foundation (on the site where Frank Lloyd Wright's house should have been built), at the beginning of the Rio Novo, where it opens into the Grand Canal, between Palazzo Balbi and Ca' Foscari.

XVIII

To Ariana Curtis
May *4th* [1893]   Lucerne, Hôtel National
(Dartmouth Ms.)

Dear Mrs. Curtis.

very delightful, very kind, very sad, and very all but
irresistible is your generous letter. To such a letter there
is but one decorous answer, an immediate dash off to
Venice and splash at the Barbaro steps. This is all the
more present to me as the ideal, as I am, for my torment,
so far on the road to Italy. But I am obliged, this time,
to recognize, with whatever gnashing of teeth, that my
individual milestone sticks hatefully up at this spot. I
got here but yesterday, and here I must stay—*pour des
raisons de famille* and very pleasant ones indeed, I should
add, for some three weeks to come. Other reasons of
the same order will then, I fear, compel my return to
England[1]. This place is admirable just now—I mean
more admirable than ever—in the first splendour of
Summer. The weather, however, I fear, is going at last
to break—and then more questions will come up.
Please believe how much I am touched by the patience
of your—both of your—hospitality. Oh, I see, I plan,
innumerable ingenious ways of enjoying it in the future.
I think with a sort of personal pang, although I didn't
know him, of poor forever-silent Symonds,[2] who will

131

enjoy it no more. This vanished apparition will indeed be a resource the less for you and you will sometimes see his ghost (with Browning's audible spectre) in the bright Venetian air. Poor, grotesque little Pen—and poor sacrificed little Mrs. Pen. There seems but one way to be sane in this queer world, but there are many ways of being mad! and a palazzo-madness is almost as alarming—or as convulsive—as an earthquake—which indeed it essentially resembles. I shall send you in a fortnight or so a better little book of tales[3] than that of the other day. I grieve greatly to hear that Mrs. Bronson is to return ill. I shall write to her within this week. I hear from Miss Woolson with great pleasure of her chance of the Pardelli apartment, such a chance for her as it strikes me—that I only fear that she may lose it by the intensity of her deliberation. Please don't let her if you can help it. *I* would make but one gulp of it. Happy Ralph—tell him, please, from me, that his life is my ideal,—by which I mean the mixture of the inner elements (though the outer are not to be despised,) that *makes* his life. But I envy *every* element of which the Barbaro is the home, and I am, dear Mrs. Curtis, of its padroni

the very affectionate friend

Henry James

NOTES

1. James went briefly to Switzerland to see his brother William and his family. He returned to London due to his theatre engagements (Edel, *The Middle Years*, p.337).

2. John Addington Symonds (1840–1893), the British writer and art historian, the author of *The History of the Renaissance in Italy* (1875–1886). He died in Rome on April 19, 1893, after spending many years at Davos, because of his tubercolosis. An aesthete and a homosexual, his life is brilliantly reconstructed by Phyllis Grosskurth.

3. The volume of tales already sent could be *The Real Thing*, that was published in March 1893, and the promised one *The Private Life*, that came out on June 3, 1893.

XIX

To Ariana Curtis
July 14*th* [1893]   2 Wellington Crescent
(Edel III)   Ramsgate

Dear Mrs. Curtis.

I rejoiced to hear from you the other day, even
though it was to gather that you have been under a
misconception as regards what must have seemed to
you an attitude (on my part) of really criminal levity
on the subject of the beloved Venice. No such levity
was intended; I haven't been heartlessly toying with its
affections; and the case is less hopeless, thank heaven,
than you perhaps suppose. I expressed myself clumsily
to Miss Woolson in appearing to intimate that I was
coming there to "live." I can only, for all sorts of
practical reasons, *live* in London, and must always keep
an habitation "mounted" there. But whenever I have
been in Venice (especially the last two or three times),
I have felt the all but irresistible desire to put my hand
on some modest *pied-à-terre* there—modest enough
to be compatible with the retention of my London
place, which is rather expensive; and such as I might
leave standing empty for months together—without
scruple—in my absence, and deposit superfluous
luggage in, when I wished to "visit" Italy. This humble

dream I still cherish—but it is most vivid when I'm on the spot—i.e. Venice; it fades a little when I'm not there. The next time I am there I shall probably act in harmony with it—and then find myself unable (such are the tricks of fate) to occupy the place for a long time afterwards. But *pazienza*; and above all more thanks than I express to you for having taken an interest in the sordid little inquiry. I think it will be a part of the fun to pursue it myself on the spot; and as it would be a question of a lowly rental (£50 a year, I fear, is my limit—one can get a palatial country bower—with a garden—for that here), there will not be the same narrowness of choice as in the case of something smart. *Basta*—and again all thanks. I have the fondest hope of going to Italy next winter—but I am learning by stern experience not to make hard and fast plans. It is only the unexpected that happens—nevertheless I fear I shall never go to India. That is only the *délassement* of leisure and fortune. The most I can hope to do is to be there to send you off—with mingled reluctance and benedictions. But these things are vague. I am very sorry indeed Miss Woolson has trouble in finding a house, or a piano. But I had an idea she wanted—I think she does want—to abide for a winter experimentally, first, in a *quartiere mobiliato*[1]. I am far from the madding crowd,[2] beside these sordid sands. There *is* a crowd, but it's vulgar and comfortable, and the air is as destitute of an edge as the language of an *h*. How charming your young lovers, and what a pleasure to have such frames to offer to such tableaux! Yours dear Mrs. Curtis and the Paron's always devotedly

Henry James

NOTES

1. Furnished flat.

2. An evident echo of the title of one of the novels of Thomas Hardy, on whom James wrote more than once.

XX

To Francis Boott
October 21*st* 1893   34 De Vere Gardens
(Edel III)

My dear Francis.

I have one of your gentle gossamer screeds again to thank you for. I enjoy the Tuscan tradition of letter-paper a shade less painfully as a reader than as a writer. Does Ann[1] stuff it into the pockets of her little Bersaglieri? I am delighted the dear little boy has assumed his national costume. The wasted exiles on the Waltham road (those whom their situation *piace poco)* must snatch him up and embrace him. You wrote from the legendary Lenox, which (though I have seen Naples and survived) I am evidently destined to descend into the tomb without having beheld. I feel all the same as if I had been brought up on the glory of it by Mrs. Tappan[2]. *Io so che sia morta, poveretta!* I lately came home from a summer of British sea-sides, which are all right if one can choose them vulgar enough, for then they are delightfully full of people one doesn't know (unless one is vulgar oneself, which of course *may* be). I am glad the sight of you in Cambridge has gilded again the Williams' American fetters. They were here long enough for me to miss them now in their *éloignement*. But the London autumn is always convenient to me, and I shall support existence here until—some time in the spring, I may be free to peregrinate to "Tuscany". I shall take Venetia by the way and pay a visit to our excellent friend Fenimore. She has taken, for the winter, Gen. de Horsey's Casa Semitecolo[3], near the Pal[azzo] Dario, and I believe is materially comfortable; especially as she loves Venice, for which small blame to her! But I figure her as extremely exhausted (as she always is at such times), with her writing and re-writing of her last novel—a great success, I believe, in relation to the particular public (a very wide American one) that she addresses. She is to have, I trust, a winter of bookless peace. The Curtises, you probably know, are just leaving for India (what ever-greenness!) and their withdrawal (as they have been most kind to her), will make the Venice winter rather bare, I fear. A' propos of which things I hear that the bloated Rezzonico is offered for sale, with all Pen Browning's hideous luxuries—except, I believe, the "Tuscan" model whom he has taken to his side in place of his truly unfortunate wife. For a poet's double child (or a double poets') he is singularly prosy. I rejoice in the good you tell me of Lizzie's boy, and long for the day when I may take him by the hand. Shan't you bring him over soon for indispensable initiations and pilgrimages? Give him, please, the love of one who loved his mother. I hope Duveneck's admirable work is now adequately known. Does not a train of solicitation follow on this? I hope he is in some stable equilibrium; and send him cordial greetings. What will become of my books when you stop reading them? They will droop; but on the other hand the American home will bloom again. Spurn it—sacrifice me first. You wouldn't scruple if you knew how I hate everything I've ever written. *Stia bene*. Yours, dear Francis, evermore

Henry James

NOTES

1. Ann, Mary Shenstone, the nanny of Francis Boott's daughter, Lizzie, for forty years. She made a gift of a "bersagliere" uniform to Lizzie's son, as recalled by Francis Boott in *Recollections of Francis Boott for his Grandson F.B.D.*, Boston, The Southgate Press, 1912, p.59.

2. Caroline Sturgis Tappan (1819–1888), of Boston, a Transcendentalist poet and a friend of Margaret Fuller, and the old friend of Henry's father and of Henry himself, who wrote of her, remembering her humour and intelligence, in *Notes of a Son and Brother*, as Edel mentions *(Letters* III, p.437).

3. The former Gothic Palazzo Orio, on the Grand Canal, near the Salute.

XXI

To Katherine de Kay Bronson
February 2nd 1894   34 De Vere Gardens W.
(Edel III)

Dear Katrina Bronson.

I have thought of you often ever since the horror of
last week—and in writing to Edith [Bronson], which I
have repeatedly done, have felt almost as if the words
reached *you* as well. I came within an ace of seeing
you, for I was twice on the very verge of rushing off
to Italy. My first knowledge of Miss Woolson's[1] death
was by a cable from her sister in New York telling
me only that fact and *asking* me to go. I made instant
preparation, but a few hours later heard, afresh—from
New York—that Miss Carter[2] was already on the
spot—and then, before night, both from Miss Carter
herself and from Baldwin, dissuasively in regard to
coming. Later, I prepared to start for Rome—to her
funeral—but at the very moment heard, for the first
time, of the unimagined and terrible manner of her
death—which sickened and overwhelmed me so,
on the spot, that I had no heart for the breathless,
sleepless rush that I had before me to reach Rome in
time. So I have been kept away from you—and I can't,
while the freshness of such a misery as it all must have
been is in the air, feel anything but that Venice is not

a place I want *immediately* to see. I had known Miss Woolson for many years and was extremely attached to her—she was the gentlest and tenderest of women, and full of intelligence and sympathy. But she was a victim to morbid melancholia, and one's friendship for her was always half anxiety. The worst mine had ever made me fear, however, was far enough from the event of which you must still be feeling the inexpressible shock. It was an act, I am convinced, of definite, irresponsible, delirious insanity, determined by illness, fever as to its form, but springing, indirectly, out [of] a general depression which, though not visible to people who saw her socially, casually, had essentially detached her from the wish to live. But it is all too pitiful and too miserable to dwell on—too tragic and too obscure. You were so close to it that it must have filled all the air of your life for several days—and this publicity of misery, this outward horror and *chiasso* round her death, was the thing in the world most alien to her and most inconceivable of her—and therefore, to my mind, most conclusive as to her having undergone some violent cerebral derangement. Nothing could be more incongruous with the general patience, reserve and dainty dignity, as it were, of her life. Save her deafness, she had absolutely no definite or unusual thing (that I know of) to minister to her habitual depression; she was free, independent, successful—

very successful indeed as a writer—and *liked*, peculiarly, by people who knew her. She had near relations who adored her and who were in a position to do much for her—especially as she was fond of them. But it was all reduced to ashes by the fact that a beneficent providence had elaborately constructed her to suffer. I can't be sufficiently grateful that Edith had the blessed inspiration of placing with her that competent and excellent Miss Holas[3]. I have just had, from Rome, a long letter from Miss Carter—for whose nearness and prompt arrival I am also devoutly thankful. What she tells me is very interesting and touching, but it doesn't penetrate the strange obscurity of so much of the matter. But that has indeed the im . . .[4] distant date. Believe me meanwhile always affectionately yours

Henry James

NOTES

1. Constance Fenimore Woolson committed suicide on January 24, 1894, throwing herself out of the window.

2. Grace Carter, the cousin of Miss Woolson, arriving from Monaco (Edel, *The Middle Years*, p.357)

3. Maria Holas, a lady who gave Italian lessons to Mrs. Gardner and who was very helpful in general.

4. Part of the ms. is missing (Edel, *Letters* III, p.467).

XXII

To Katherine de Kay Bronson
Tuesday 20*th* March [1894]   Grand Hôtel de Gênes:
(Edel III)   Genoa

My dear Katrina B.

Will you render an old friend a very gentle service—
such a service as may accelerate the hour at which
he shall find himself at your feet? A combination of
circumstances, some of which I would have wished
other, but which I must accept (I am speaking of
course quite apart from the question of *inclination*, and
intense desire to see you),[1] make it absolutely necessary
I should be in Venice from the 1st April. This being
the case, as I have work in hand, I must get into some
quiet and comfortable material conditions—and I
peculiarly detest the Venetian hotels: loathe in fact
to be in a hotel, in Venice, even for a day. It occurs
to me that the apartment occupied by Miss Woolson
last summer before she went to Casa Semitecolo and
which I believe she found very comfortable, may be
free and obtainable—or if not the other set of rooms
in the same house. But I have forgotten the address
and don't know the woman's name. I only seem to
remember vaguely that the house was *Casa Biondetti*[2]
and that it's quite near where Paul Tilton used to live.
The Hohenlohes, or some such people, had occupied

the rooms before Miss Woolson. You will probably easily identify the place, and what service I ask of your great kindness is to go and see if one of the apartments *is* free. If so I think I should like to take it from Sunday or Monday next—for a month, with liberty to renew; that is if the woman will give it to me on the same terms on which she gave it to Miss Woolson and will *cook* for me as she did for her. (I have ceased, in my old age, to be able to prowl about for my food.) I don't at all know what Miss W. paid—but I remember her mentioning in a letter that the *padrona* "did" for her very well. Should you be able to cause this inquiry to be made the day you receive this—and should you then be able to address me here a few lines of information? If dear Edith had got back I would appeal directly to *her* kindness in the matter—and her more violent activity. But I shall thank you with all my heart. It is delicious to me to think I shall see you, dear Katrina B., so very soon. I arrived here but a couple of days ago and shall be here till I go to Venice; where I trust I shall find you in all respects at your ease—or as much so as we worried mortals ever can be. I suppose Edith is well on her way home by this. I saw less of her in London than I desired, but I shall make it up in Casa Alvisi. I shall make *everything* up in Casa Alvisi.

Casa Curtis, I suppose, is empty for another two or three weeks?—If Casa Biondetti (if that be its name) is all occupied, I will come on, at the same date, and simply go to the Britannia till I can find something—unless by chance you beneficently know and are able graciously to suggest, something like the place I speak of—and as good. A word from you at any rate will rejoice my heart and add wings to my approach. This place is charming and the sense of recovered Italy inexpressibly dear to me. There is nothing like it. *Stia bene—sempre bene.* I can't tell you how happy I am to be able to try to say to you "à bientôt!" Yours, my dear old friend, very tenderly

Henry James

P.S. If by a miracle *both* the apartments should be free I should like, I think, the better one—if there is a difference, even if it be not the one Miss Woolson had.

NOTES

1. Parenthesis added (Edel, *Letters* III, p.469).

2. Casa Biondetti, on the Grand Canal, where the painter Rosalba Carriera had lived (as marked by a plaque). It is on the right of Palazzo Venier dai Leoni (The Guggenheim Collection), looking from the water.

XXIII

To Isabella Stewart Gardner
June 29*th* [1894]   Venice, Casa Biondetti
(I.S.G.M. Ms.)

Dearest Mrs. Gardner,

I tried to write to you yesterday from Asolo—for *auld long syne*; but the "view" got so between me and my paper that I couldn't get round the purple mountains to dip my pen. I have just been spending three days there with Mrs. Bronson—alone with her and Edith— three days of great loveliness. In Venice I have been spending 3 months and I depart in less than a week. It breaks my heart to say it, but therefore I shall not be here when you hold sway at the Barbaro in September and October. I am not even very sure I shall *ever* be here again. Venice, to tell the truth, has been simply blighted, and made a proper little hell (I mean what I say!) by "people"! They have flocked here, these many weeks, in their thousands, and life has been a burden in consequence. The Barbaro is lovelier than ever—but what's the use? I return to England some- time—early—in August—and hide behind a Swiss mountain till then. Shall you not be in London after I am back? I suppose you are, perversely, just arriving there now. Bien du plaisir! I shall follow you up—in

imagination—the rest of the summer!
Yours most affectionately,

Henry James

XXIV

To Ariana Wormeley Curtis
20*th* April [1897]   34, De Vere Gardens, W.
(Dartmouth Ts.)

My dear Mrs. Curtis,

This is to thank you and D.S.C. as well (that appellation reminds me—very properly *du reste*—of L.S.D.) for two graceful tributes of these latter days. I am glad to know—very—that Osborne[1] and his daughter have given you reassurance and have scoured the lagoon to their general benefit. As for mine—my general benefit, don't pity me for my lame wrist, which is a combination of native imbecility and acquired rheumatism, but which is also what is called a blessing in disguise; inasmuch as it has made me renounce for ever the manual act, which I hate with all the hatred of a natural inaptitude, and have renounced for ever, to devote myself in every particular to dictation. The latter does not hamper me at all: in letters quite the reverse, and in commerce with the Muse so little that I foresee the day when it will be a pure luxury. I am practising it now at a rate that I must put forward as my excuse for delays from week to week to start for your *parages*. The absolute necessity of finishing a biggish job has held me; and another bribe has been these delicious Easter holidays, just, alas, closing, which, by making London a desert contribute to the holy calm and charm of the month of April. I fear I shall not get off before May 5th, which, alas, gives me the drawback of so reduced a time near you before the hot weather, which I bear in Italy so ill, begins to rage. I am afraid I shall be able to put in but three or four days in Venice and three or four days at Asolo— where my interest in the new property will be greater than my interest in the old scandals. I rejoice that you come early to England, and shall be back almost as soon as you arrive—that is in time to welcome you. I renew my thanks to L.S.D. for his kind note and beg that he will consider this small corner of the present a temporary acknowledgement of it. Poor Howard Potter, yes—I dined with him, at the Bayard's-not many weeks previous, when I thought he looked ominously ill. Ce que c'est que de nous! I am delighted that I shall find Ralph in Venice. I too pause, en route, at the feet of the Ranee. I bless your house, and all that it contains—not least the ghost, or what prevails there of the presence, of the noble Pisani. There ought, for her, to be no decline, but a kind of swift immersion—into the Adriatic, say, of Almorò[2] and his Doges. Yours, dear Mrs. Curtis, evermore,

Henry James

NOTES

1. Osborne Curtis (1858–1918), the younger son of Daniel and Ariana Curtis.

2. Almorò Pisani, the husband of Evelin van Millingen, was the last heir of the great Pisani family of Santo Stefano, which had given one doge, Alvise (1735–1741) to the Republic of Venice.

XXV

To Ariana Wormeley Curtis
October 30*th*, 1898   Rye, Lamb House
(Dartmouth Ms.)

Dear Mrs. Curtis.

Your noble, your magnificent present followed, after a few days, the so interesting letter in which you announced it, and I ought already to have sent on its way this assurance of my *really* immense, my affectionate, gratitude. The admirable object reached me in perfect safety and packed with a science worthy of its luster and its history: nothing could have been more complete—so that I almost felt at first that I really ought to keep the jewel in its casket. It is a brave and brilliant jewel, and I can't tell you how handsome and picturesque I think it, nor how it gives "importance", as the connoisseurs say, to the whole side of the room on which it so discreetly glitters. I have placed it above the chimney-piece (after trying other postures,) and it consorts beautifully with the tone of the wall. It has— the so far-descended metal has, a delightful mildness, a silvering, of yellow. *Moltissime grazie*! I sit through everything—and there is plenty, isn't there?—very firm here. My present notion is to stay till Christmas, and then go abroad—but I have so often and so horribly belied these intimations that I don't dare to make them. Only I *do* most ardently hope to go. The beauty of this little old place all this October has been extreme—beauty of colour and atmosphere, sky, sea, sunsets, distances—nearnessess too—and I am freshly sorry you happened to see it in a hot prosaic glare which did it no justice. Yet what matter to you, children of the Veronese, our poor little echoes of Constable and Cotman?[1] You are re-bathed in glory, and what fun your re-integration of [the] Barbaro domicile must have been! I walked with you in imagination up the steps and fondly pattered beside you—between you—along the Sala and into the incredible drawing-room the first time you reassured yourselves of them. I have had, these last weeks, rather too many inmates—that I hope *you* haven't. I've had however for the last fortnight a very pleasant and interesting young one in the person of Jonathan Sturges[2]—originally of New York, a friend of Ralph's and of thousands of others besides. Half my time is spent in devouring the papers for their interest and the other half in hating them for the horrible way in which they envenomize all dangers and reverberate all lies. As the army is quite clearly the one thing left *debout* in France it *will* presumably soon have its new Caesar—by acclamation—in the person of the younger of the Bonaparte Princes—but I thank my stars that the military justice of France is not the régime it's my fate to live under. They would make short work with it here. But dear old *dramatic* France—may she never lack scenarios: so long as I am in the boxes. A great gale blows here, my chimney roars and even shakes, and my garden shakes off in each gust some article of clothing. Meanwhile, I imagine you are eating grapes and figs in yours. I bless you for the news of Mrs. Bronson's "real" betterness. I bless you both for all other things besides and am, dear Mrs. Curtis, yours very constantly

Henry James

NOTES

1. John Constable (1776–1837) and John S. Cotman (1782–1842), the British painters.

2. Jonathan Sturges (1864–1909), American. He lived for a long time in London, although impaired by polio as a child. See Edel, *Letters* III, p.435.

XXVI

To Ariana and Daniel Curtis
March 16*th*, 1899   Rye, Lamb House
(Dartmouth Ms.)

Very dear Curtises Both.

I am deeply in debt to both of you—renewedly within a day or two; and, verily, if I've never acknowledged till this late hour a beautiful communication of many weeks ago, it is because I was fairly ashamed to write again, from my fireside, that I was "coming"—eternally coming—without giving any proof of being on my way. I wanted to wait till I could give that proof—tiresomely—delayed—though also calculatingly—from week to week; and now at last here it *is*. I've been in Paris a week and I leave for *patria nostra* about on the 21st or 22nd. I stop, however, three days at Costebelle to redeem a rigid vow to the Bourgets, and three more to redeem at Bogliasco a pledge of a softer order to the Ranee. Then, with a long precaution, I risk myself on Italian soil. Your enumeration of the social features of Rome, I confess, *terrifies* me, and my real hanging back till now has been from this same dread of the collected People—the terrible Popular Romance of whom, all winter, rumour has represented to me the multitude. It's exactly to escape them *all* that I am cultivating the cunning of the Choctaw and if need be the rudeness of the Apache. Five years ago they were the ruination of Italy to *me*, and the reason why I have suffered these five years of privation to roll by. I *have* to go to Rome, absolutely, by reason of a gouged-out promise—of old date, too old, now—to the Waldo Storys[1]; and were it not for this I should hug, exclusively, the minor and unfashionable towns. But forgive this churlish tone— which is the less graceful as I find Paris at present more empty than I have *ever* known it. My old circle here has faded away into the Ewigkeit—though there are always cousins—little female cousins so ready to be taken about. I *dined* three last night and took them to the Français[2]—Most kind thanks for your anxiety about my fire. Yes, it was a horrid little scare—but only two rooms were compromised (above and below,) and reparation, amended and scientific reconstruction, is already under way. I was *up*, fortunately, though it was four-thirty a.m; I had arranged everything to come to Folkestone and that on the morrow, crossing hither the next day; and I was having a vigil of procrastinated letters and other such jobs: otherwise I don't know what of sickening might have overwhelmed me. Smouldering fire broke out under the floor, communicated from treacherous antique fireplace— and woodwork—construction, and burnt *downwards* into the dining room. But the brave pumpers—the little local brigade—were cool as well as prompt, and my injury by water was almost *nil*. It was a horrid night—one didn't tumble into bed till five-thirty; but it might have been much horrider. Only it kept me on there, all packed and ready to start, for two or three weeks—till I could see remedies under way. Your mention of Ralph and Mrs. Ralph here are (sic) my first knowledge of their presence and I shall certainly try to find them, and as certainly only miss them, before I leave. I ought long ago to have reported on my visit to Sargent's (in January) studio and my vision, there, of the two pictures. *But*—it's difficult. Frankly, candidly, crudely—I didn't like the portrait of Mrs. Ralph[3] *at all* and don't take it as worthy of any one concerned. I don't understand, among other things, why and how artist and husband conspired to dress her so—for, I think the dress (and I'm not speaking in the least of the *décolletage* in particular,) [neither] agreeable [n]or distinguished: indeed it seems to me that her certainly very striking beauty is of an order to rejoice in clothes the least fustian possible. The picture makes me want particularly to see her—I am sure I should admire her all the *more* after it; and I wish my days there were life remembered. The *Barbaro-saloon* thing[4], on the other hand, I absolutely and unreservedly *adored*. I can't help thinking you have a slightly fallacious impression of the effect of your (*your*, dear Mrs. Curtis,) indicated head and face. It is an indication so *sommaire* that I think it speaks entirely for itself, as a simple sketchy hint and it didn't displease me; set as it is the general beauty— the splendour—of the thing as a total rendering: I've seen few things of S[argent]'s that I've ever craved more to possess! I hope you haven't altogether let it go. If on reaching your *parages* (I mean Ventimiglia!) I get the sense of a still great plenitude in Rome, I shall rush off to see Mrs. B[ronson] at Asolo and come to Rome as soon as April or even May shall have done (if April does do,) some thriving out. Therefore it is a little uncertain yet when I shall see you. I don't quite gather when you return to the Barbaro. I greet you affectionately and am ever so faithfully yours

Henry James

P.S. March 19*th*. I have shamefully kept my letter over, because I felt I after all *should* see the Ralphs—and wanted to report of them. Well, I *have* seen them, and they have been charming to me, making me breakfast and go to wonderful old (and new) shops and collections with them—and likewise dine tonight. She is singularly handsome, to my vision, and harmonious and sympathetic—every way gentle and gracious and charming: miles beyond the infelicitous picture. It does her poor justice. I ask myself what, if she has such beauty in her now rather marked "situation" (though looking essentially *well,*) what she must normally and usually have. She is a presence in your lives on which I greatly congratulate you. Ralph is clearly happy— and their apartment admirable, lovely. But this Paris! I mean with its more and more Bazaar-Caravansery side! However, the Avenue du Bois as an opera-box (excuse the swift indications) "A. I." Forgive my delays and my delay. Also my violence about the portrait. Perhaps I should see it again. But I told her how much better I liked her. A' bientôt. Yours again

H.J.

NOTES

1. James went to Rome because Waldo Story, the son of sculptor William Wetmore Story, who had died in 1895, had asked him to write his father's biography. James accepted, although with no enthusiasm. The result was *William Wetmore Story and His Friends* (1903), where James widened the "biography" to the whole American scene of Story's *Rome and Europe*.

2. The Français: short for Le Théatre-Français, better known as the *Comédie Française*, in the Place du Théatre-Français, near the Palais-Royal. See K. Baedeker, *Paris et ses environs*, Leipzig-Paris, 1889, p.*22*.

3. Sargent painted the portrait of Lisa as a wedding present, in 1898, see Richard Ormond, *John Singer Sargent*, London, Phaidon, 1970, p.251.

4. The painting is *An Interior in Venice* (1899). See P. Hills, *John Singer Sargent* cit., p.69 (n.44). Sargent stayed in Venice on several occasions, and had a studio in Palazzo Rezzonico in 1880–1881. In 1882 he was a guest of the Curtises at Palazzo Barbaro and painted a portrait of Mrs. Daniel Curtis (see H. Honour and J. Fleming, *The Venetian Hours of Henry James, Whistler and Sargent*, London, Walker, 1991, p.56). Sargent and Ralph Curtis had met in Paris, studying with Carolus Duran, but they were in fact related on the maternal line. In Venice Sargent and Curtis used the same model, the Venetian young woman called "Gigia" (Viani). James wrote several times on Sargent's paintings, including the famous and controversial portrait of *Madame X* (Madame Gautreau). On James's and Sargent's Venetian friends, see Rosella Mamoli Zorzi, *Browning a Venezia*, Venice, 1989.

XXVII

To Alvin Langdon Coburn[1]
December 6*th* 1906   Rye, Lamb House
(Edel IV)

Dear Alvin Langdon!

I have just written to Miss Constance Fletcher,[2] in
Venice where she lives, at periods (with her infirm old
mother and her mother's second husband, Eugene
Benson, also I fear invalidical and a little played-out, but
a painter of refined and interesting little landscapes of
the Venetian country), in the *Palazzo Cappello, Rio Marin*;
which is the old house I had more or less in mind for
that of the Aspern Papers. I have told her exactly what
I want you to do, outside and in, and as she is a very
kind and very artistic person, you can trust yourself to
her completely for guidance. She will expect you, and
will, I am sure, respond to my request on your behalf
in a cordial and sympathetic spirit. Your best way to
get to the Rio Marin will be to obtain guidance, for a
few coppers, from some alert Venetian street-boy (or
of course you can go, romantically, in a gondola). But
the extremely tortuous and complicated walk—taking
Piazza San Marco as a starting point—will show you
so much, so many bits and odds and ends, such a revel
of Venetian picturesqueness, that I advise your doing
it on foot as much as possible. You go almost as if you

were going to the Station to come out at the end of the bridge opposite to the same. Now that I think of it indeed your very best way, for shortness, will be to go by the Vaporetto, or little steamboat, which plies every few minutes on the Grand Canal, straight to the Stazione, and there, crossing the big contiguous iron bridge, walk to Rio Marin in three or four minutes. It is the old faded pink-faced, battered-looking and quite homely and plain (as things go in Venice) old Palazzino on the right of the small Canal, a little way along, as you enter it by the end of the Canal towards the Station. It has a garden behind it, and I think, though I am not sure, some bit of a garden-wall beside it; it doesn't moreover bathe its steps, if I remember right, directly in the Canal, but has a small paved Riva or footway in front of it, and *then* water-steps down from this little quay. As to that, however, the time since I have seen it may muddle me; but I am almost sure. At any rate anyone about will identify for you Ca' Cappello, which is familiar for Casa C; *casa*, for your ingenuous young mind, meaning House and being used, save for the greatest palaces, as much as palazzo. You must judge for yourself, face to face with the object, how much, on the spot, it seems to lend itself to a picture. I think it *must*, more or less, or sufficiently; with or without such adjuncts of the rest of the scene (from the bank opposite, from the bank near, or from wherever you can damnably manage it) as may seem to contribute or complete—to be needed, in short, for the interesting effect. I advise you to present your note first—unless you are so much in the humor the moment you arrive in front of the place as to want then and there to strike off something at a heat. My friends will help you by any suggestion or indication whatever, and will be very intelligent about it; and will let you see if something be not feasible from the Garden behind; which also figures a bit in the story. What figures most is the big old Sala, the large central hall of the principal floor of the house, to which they will introduce you, and from which from the large, rather bare Venetian perspective of which, and preferably looking toward the garden-end, I very much hope some result. In one way or another, in fine, it seems to me it ought to give something. If it doesn't, even with the help of more of the little canal-view etc., yield satisfaction, wander about until you find something that looks sufficiently like it, some old second-rate palace on a by-canal, with a Riva in front, and if any such takes you at all, do it at a venture, as a possible alternative. But get the Sala at Ca' Cappello, without fail, if *it* proves at all manageable or effective.

For the other picture, that of *The Wings*, I had vaguely in mind the Palazzo Barbaro, which you can see very well from the first, the upper, of the iron bridges, the one nearest the mouth of the Grand Canal, and which crosses from Campo San Stefano to the great Museum of the Academy. The palace is the very old Gothic one, on your right, just before you come to the iron bridge, after leaving (on the vaporetto) the steamboat-station of the Piazza. Only one palace, the Franchetti, a great big sort of yellow-faced restored one, with vast Gothic windows and balcony, intervenes between it and the said iron bridge. The Barbaro has its water-steps beside it, as it were; that is a little gallery running beside a small stretch of side-canal. But in addition it also has fine water-steps (I remember!) to the front door of its lower apartment. (The side-steps I speak of belong to the apartment with the beautiful range of old *upper* Gothic windows, those attached to the part of the palace concerned in my story.) But I don't propose you should attempt here anything but the outside; and you must judge best if you can rake the object most effectively from the bridge itself, from the little campo in front of the Academy, from some other spot further—that is further toward the Salute, or from a gondola (if your gondolier can keep it steady enough) out on the bosom of the Canal. If none of these positions yield you something you feel to be effective, try some other palace, or simply try some other right range of palaces, in some other reach or stretch of the Canal; ask Miss Fletcher to please show you, to this end, what I have written to her about that. And do any other odd and interesting bit you can, that may serve for a sort of symbolised and generalised Venice in case everything else fails; preferring the noble and fine aspect, however, to the merely shabby and familiar (as in the case of those views you already have)—yet especially *not* choosing the pompous and obvious things that one everywhere sees photos of. I hope this will be, with my very full letter to Miss Fletcher, enough to provide for all your questions. I will write the note to Miss F. to-night and send it on to you tomorrow. Let me know when, having seen Pinker again, you start. Indeed if you will give me two or three days notice I will send you the note to Miss F. *then*, in preference; as my letter, posted to her today, may bring a reply *before* you start—in which case I might have to write a fourth communication! Yours,

Henry James

P.S. It will much help if you will take two or three subjects to *show* to Miss Fletcher and Benson: the Porte-Cochère ("American")—the St. John's Wood Villa—the antique-shop, Portland Place etc.—or my Hall (for an interior). H.J.

NOTES

1. Alvin Langdon Coburn (1882–1966), American photographer. He was entrusted with the twenty-four frontispieces of James's New York Edition (1906–1907). He had photographed Henry James for the *Century Magazine* in 1905. In his *Autobiography* Coburn tells how simple and wonderful it was to work with James, looking for the places to photograph. James knew exactly what he wanted. A propos *The Aspern Papers*, in his letter of December 9, 1908 James insisted: "I want Casa Cappello . . ." The photographs mentioned in the P.S. concern *The American*, as indicated, *The Tragic Muse* (St. John's Wood house), *The Golden Bowl* (Portland Place), see Edel, *Letters* IV, p.431, The Master, pp.333–339. A. L. Coburn, *An Autobiography*, edited by H. and A. Gersheim, New York, Dover, 1978, p.52.

2. Constance Fletcher (1858–1938), an American writer who lived in Italy. Using the pseudonym "George Fleming" she published stories and novels, among which was *Kismet, A Nile Novel* (1877), which was a great success. Fletcher was not liked by the Anglo-American society living in Italy. Neither the Gurtises nor Miss Woolson liked her. James, however, must have liked her, and also Gertrude Stein later, who met her at Villa Curonia, at Mabel Dodge's. The reason why Fletcher was not appreciated was partly linked to her mother's initially "irregular" position: "When Constance was 12 years old her mother fell in love with the English tutor of Constance's younger brother. Constance knew that her mother was about to leave her home. For a week Constance lay on her bed and wept and then she accompanied her mother and her future stepfather to Italy." "When Constance was 18 years old she wrote a bestseller called *Kismet* and was engaged to be married to Lord Lovelace the descendant of Byron. She did not marry him and thereafter lived always in Italy", see Gertrude Stein, *The*

Autobiography of Alice B. Toklas (1933), in *Selected Writings*, edited by C. Van Vechten, New York, Vintage, 1962, p.122. Eugene Benson (1839–1908), Constance's stepfather, was a painter who often participated in the Biennial Expositions of Venice, where he lived, in Ca' Cappello.

XXVIII

To Jessie Allen[1]
Monday June 24*th* 1907   Palazzo Barbaro
(Edel IV)   Canal Grande, Venezia

Dear brave and ever-prized Goody.

You will wonder what has been "becoming" of me—
but not more, with my prolonged absence, than I have
wondered what has been becoming of myself. I am at
last on the near "home stretch," and I yearn for that
goal—but though I shall thus see you the sooner I feel
that I shan't be able to meet you with any clearness of
conscience unless I shall have made you a sign from
these ever adorable (*never* more so!) marble halls and
sent you some echo of our inimitable Barbarites—
who are quite as inimitable as ever. I came here five
days ago—from a week in Florence and previous
month, almost, in Rome and Naples—all of which
time Ariana was pulling awfully hard at one end of
my scant tether. I am now the only guest—the full-
blown summer is divine (even if pretty torrid), D.
and A. are kindness and hospitality unlimited (or
limited only by my condemnation to *sneaking* relations
with everyone else—it would *never* be possible, on
this ground, for me to stay here again); and in short
Venice is really (thanks to the glow and large ease
of the season) more characteristically exquisite and

loveable than I've ever known it. I have this vast cool upper floor—all scirocco draughts and easy undressedness quite to myself; I go out with Ariana at 5, in the cool (comparative), and then again by moonlight; so that if I'm not madly in love with her what influence is wanting? Dan'l visits the matutinal Lido in the torrid A.M. hours—just as of yore—but if he yearns, yearns in vain for my society. Angelo the everlasting has his white-gloved forefinger (as of yore) on almost every morsel that goes down my throat, and Angelino, worthy offshoot of such a scion, gets my hat off my head and my stick out of my fond clutch almost before I'm half up the grand staircase. So you see the dear old Barbarism is an element undefiled and uncorrupted—and that every note strikes true from the cool dim dawn, when the canal is a great curly floor of dark green marble, to the still cooler blue night when I go forth with my Lady to be cradled by the plash outside the Giudecca. But of all this I must tell you—and of the new heartbreak it is just only to feel this enchantress (I allude now to the terrible old Venice herself!) weave her spell just again supremely to lose her. One dreams again so of some clutched perch of one's own here. But it's the most drivelling of dreams. Our friends leave for England on the 29th and I the day before—next Friday. I go to Milan and Lausanne (by the Simplon orifice) and then to Paris—Dover—Rye. I come up to town for three or four days about July 12th. Then for a jaw! Such a fine old feast as it will be to see you—and I allude neither to lunch nor to dinner. You will probably even see D. and A. first. That is best! Forgive this mere scrap of a hand-wag from your faithful old

Henry James

NOTE

1. Elisabeth Jessie Allen (1845–1918), of a noble British family, was introduced to James by the Curtises at Palazzo Barbaro in 1899. James made friends with the lively lady, who was a brilliant talker and letter writer, and would send him excessively wonderful presents for Christmas. After the gift of two bear skins, which James did not want to accept, the two friends made a deal: James accepted the gift, on the condition that he would call her "Goody-Two-Shoes" for the rest of his life. The name was that of an XVIII century story, attributed to Oliver Goldsmith, which told about a poor orphan girl who owned one shoe only and was given another shoe (see also, *Letters* IV, p.153; *The Master*, pp.151–156). See also H. James, *Letters to Miss Allen*, Rosella Mamoli Zorzi ed., Milan, Archinto, 1993.

Scirocco by Ralph Curtis

LETTERS BY THE CURTISES

I

Ariana Curtis to Mary Curtis[1]
October 27*th* [1883]   Venice, Palazzo Barbaro
(Marciana Ms.)

My dear Mary.

Now you must be back in Boston—and I daresay you
are glad to be at home, after so long battling with the
foe in the shape of hotel keepers, etc. I am sorry you
are so far off. Nothing especial here—The weather
celestial, and no thought of winter—fires only in the
evening, for cheerfulness' sake. The *vendemmia* is over
at the Vendramin[2]. The grapes all cut, only a lingering
few still left for the table. We are now about to make
plantations of rhododendrons, mahonias, and such,
in place of the cabbages of this year. The old days of
Chest[nut] Hill planting seem renewed—and I hold
trees while the earth is shovelled over their roots—
rien n'est changé que le nom du jardinier—Domenico
D'Este instead of Nelson Stevens, or Otis P. Norcross.
The certainty of success with young trees is also a
comfortable change—we shall not see our darlings

171

wizzle in the icy Northwest blast. You must have arrived in time to drink Johnny Lowell's health on his wedding day[3]. Much love and congrat[ulation]s to dear Lucy, and to Johnny when you see him. We have seen a good deal of the Brownings since they have been here. Now they are going to Greece with Mrs. Bronson[4].

There were *beautiful* tableaux the other night at Mrs. B[ronson]'s, arranged by Duveneck, who appeared himself as the Bravo of Venice[5]—in four *tableaux*—wrapped in his cloak, sharpening his sword, giving the blow—and lastly wiping the fatal weapon. It was tremendous—and made real blood run cold. Afety was in powder and satin—18th century—very pretty—and also as an "Incroyable". The best was perhaps Laura Mocenigo, a beautiful blonde, as Titian's daughter—holding the basket of fruit over her head—pearls in her blonde hair, and a nice old brocade gown. Even poor little I was dragged off at a minute's notice, and made to appear as a Vandyke, with a great fraise pinned onto my gown, which luckily was black satin with a square neck. Miss Ker as her grandmother by Romney[6] was beautiful. They were far better than any I ever saw, although got up with hardly any preparation—Duveneck is a great hand at them.

I never got any Spanish books, nor the "Queen"

nor *Journal des Modes*; did get *A. Peto*[7]. I therefore owe you the following enclosed list. I had a note from Sara G[reenough][8]. She has gone back to Rome. Nina keeps on well. She says they are anxious about Alfred who has not been heard of since May—and has drawn no money. Is that true? No Americans here now; but many English. A very nice Miss Barbara Lyall seems to make a friend of me. Last Saturday we had a roomfull, and but two Am[erican]s. We don't know yet where we shall go for winter

Ariana

NOTES

1. Mary Curtis, born on March 15, 1827, was the sister of Daniel Sargent Curtis (Mass. Vital Records, Boston, Births 1810–1849, vol. VIII, microfiche 62, Oxford, Mass., Holbrook Research Institute, 1985).

1. The Curtises had the garden of the Vendramin on the Giudecca, where they went in their gondola.

3. Perhaps one of the brothers of Percival Lowell, the famous astronomer, who was a friend of Ralph Curtis with whom he travelled to Japan in 1891 and to Algeria in 1895.

4. The project was not carried out.

5. The Bravo of Venice was a very popular subject in nineteenth century historical novels and paintings, including James Fenimore Cooper's *The Bravo* (1831), and Meissonnier's *The Two Bravos*.

6. *Mrs. Ker*, see H. Ward and W. Roberts, *Romney*, London, Agnew, 1904, vol. II, p.88.

7. Ariana is referring to the novel *Altiora Peto*, by Laurence Oliphant (1829–1888). Oliphant was a British diplomat, traveller and author of many travel books (on Jordan, China, Japan, Palestine, Nepal, Egypt etc.). He was Secretary to Lord Elgin in Washington, D.C. (1854) and in China (1857–1859) and Japan. The Curtises, themselves great travellers to the East, must have enjoyed his works.

8. Sara Greenough: the Greenoughs were related to the Curtises because Daniel Sargent Curtis's father had married Laura Greenough (1815–1851), as a second bride. Laura was the sister of the sculptor Horatio Greenough (1807–1883)

II

Daniel Sargent Curtis to Mary Curtis
October 31*st* 1883   Venice
(Marciana Ms.)

Dear Mary.

We suppose you arrived, and that after all you will find Osborne there. We hope you 'scaped certain storms reported on the way and due here now—but only manifest in cirrhus. We go on thus far in lovely weather and still wear summer clothes. We may have had four or five cloudy days only since you left us; and as the garden testifies, no rain except insignificant showers. At evening now we have a little wood fire for brightness, and dine on the large round table in Ralph's salon, which is very cheery. The sun is bright and warm all day in front and as we won't shut it out, have to turn over the carpets and cover chairs with newspapers. Duveneck is painting Ralph again and we hope may succeed. Ariana has been 'at home' every Saturday, and many visitors, but this year few Americans and many English. Last Sat[urday] of a room full, only Americans were Mrs. Bronson and Duveneck. There are nice French consul and wife lately from Gibraltar where eleven years and speak English perfectly. Young people and their apartment furnished with Spanish and Moorish things. You didn't see Mme de Pilat, wife of Austrian Consul and sister of Baron Huebner, who is very nice. Brownings, of course, we have much of. They and Bronsons arranged to go to Greece next week. But *tout est rompu*. He greatly wished to go—but Miss B[rowning] hates sea and Mrs. Bronson very hard to move. So they gave it up. We had capital *tableaux vivants* arranged by Duveneck at Mrs. Bronson's. He insisted on A[riana] being a Vandyck, much approved. The great Blumenthal musical composer was there, clever handsome Jew. Also Mundellas[1]. Brownings walk every a.m. to Pub[lic] Garden and feed the Elephant. They say pomegranates made him drunk. I must take him a lot from our garden. There is a Miss Lyall of London, very [. . .] and knows all the nice folk, stays with Tennyson. She is here with Sir Alex[ander] Gordon and daughter invalid. They came on Sat[urday] evening. Live in Palace below Rialto opposite picturesque but noisy herb market, and wonderful view of Grand Canal as centre of a crescent at that point. We went for the first time to Pal[azzo] Morosini[2], close by us, inhabited by the family and permit required. Quite the best thing here, i.e. the ancient abode of ancient family, connected with most great events in history. We have letter from O[sborne] S[argent] C[urtis] today from West. So you will be sure to meet. Also from Sara G[reenough], who had letter from you. Best love to all. Affectionately ever yours

D.S.C.

NOTES

1. The family of Anthony Mundella (1825–1897), a British Member of Parliament.

2. Palazzo Morosini at Santo Stefano, quite close to Palazzo Barbaro, formerly belonging to Francesco I il Peloponnesiaco. Its sumptuous furnishing was at the time still intact. There lived in it Loredana Gatterburg Morosini, the last descendant of the Doge. On her death (1884) the grandiose collections were dispersed in an auction by the Gatterburg heirs.

III

Ariana Curtis to Mary Curtis
November 8*th* [1885]   Venice, Palazzo Barbaro
(Marciana Ms.)

My dear Mary –

I have your of October 9th [. . .] I must tell you a
secret, as I know it will interest you—and I wish you
to know it before anybody else. We have bought the
Barbaro. But the papers have not yet been signed,
and so we say nothing about it—as there are two rich
people here each looking about for a palazzo, and if
the Jew[1] who now owns it had a superior offer, I think
he is capable of throwing us over. We shall have the
whole palace, except Countess Pisani's mezzanine—
and pay 70.000 francs—about $13.500 at present rate
of exchange. This part please keep quite to yourself—
as if we should sell it again—we should ask a great deal
more. The common Italians are not at all aware of the
artistic value of such a unique specimen of decoration
of 17th century as our *gran sala*. They consider the
value as based upon the number of rooms, and the
vicinity to the Piazza. A marble-floor maker told
Angelo, it would cost 15.000 francs to make the dining
room floor now—the one with sunflowers and mother
o' pearl. We have been much exercised in our minds
for a year as to whether we should give it up when our

lease expires—but I confess to feeling somewhat like the Arab to his horse, at the thought of turning my back on the dear old place. We, however, do not intend to be tied to it—regarding it as a good investment, for there is a 'boom' in Venetian palaces, and the price will rapidly rise, if rich foreigners begin to set the fashion of buying them. We are now conducting the negotiations for a friend for one, which will make the third bought by foreigners this year.

We went up to see the floors over us. They are very nice and have view over the laguna. We shall let them to bachelors, if any desirable ones turn up, and in that way make our purchase a paying investment. The banker Blumenthal says D.S.C. has got a very valuable piece of property. We are to have a winter apartment in Rome in the house just bought by a young man named Crawshay[2], with whom Ralph has gone to Vienna. We shall not be able to have it before next winter however. It is opposite Barberini Palace. The Brownings are coming to dine today, as they often do. Mr. Browning reads his poetry to us—it is a very great pleasure. What would the Browning society people[3] give to be present! I had an afternoon party one day to hear him. We have had a great deal of company this autumn—nice people—mostly English. My receptions have been quite full and gay—tapering off now, and I think I shall soon stop. I invited general Lee's Italian fiancée last time. She is pleasing, modest, and speaks English, luckily for George who would be quite unable to declare his passion in Italian. I have had seven visitors in succession this afternoon, interrupting every time I sat down to this letter.

With much love, ever dear Mary, your affectionate sister,

Ariana

NOTES

1. Cav. Cesare Musatti, who then owned the palace thanks to his wife Sofia Cantoni, whose father, Israele Cantoni, had in turn bought it on July 7, 1875. The selling of the palace began in 1861 (April 6), when Elisa Basso, who had inherited it from Marc'Antonio Barbaro (who died September 24, 1858) sold it to Anselmo Clerlé, Isacco Jenna and Alberto Ehrenfreund. Part of the palace was sold in 1866 (24 March) to Victorine Roussel-Pardelli and her husband Giovanni Pardelli, part (two-thirds) was sold by Ehrenfreund to Lampronti and Jenna, and then to Israele Cantoni.

2. Robert Thompson Crawshay, a friend of Ralph Curtis.

3. The Browning Society was founded by F. J. Furnivall and Emily Hickey in 1881.

IV

Ariana Curtis to Mary Curtis
January 31*st* [1886]   Rome, Hôtel Victoria
(Marciana Ms.)

My dear Mary.

Daniel got your letter the other day—and we were very glad to hear—for it was such an immense time that we were afraid there was something the matter—and we were anxious to know how the Venice plan had struck you. There is no immediate need of coming to a decision—for, though we have already had several enquiries as to whether we should be willing to let the apartments upstairs, we have declined to give any answer until we have really become acquainted with the place—and know what would be most suitable for you, if you decide to come. We should also be *very* particular *indeed* about tenants—no children—no pianos. A bride and bridegroom have applied—who are to be married in June—possibly we may let them have the other apartment—as they are nice young people [. . .] We have been amused this week with an auction sale of a Spanish painter's things in the Storys' Studio building[1]. We authorised Waldo to bid for us, and strange to say, we got the very things we wanted! They are first a very curious old Spanish 1600 Cabinet called a "Bargueña"—and stand—covered outside with plaques of old iron-work—gilded—altogether a very curious and peculiar thing. Mr. Alvarez bought it out of a Convent at Oviedo. Secondly, a small Moorish Cabinet—bought in the Asturias—quite a beauty—old inlaying in Arab designs. Thirdly some pieces of old Cordovan leather, gold and silver and colours—very handsome indeed. We are to lend it to old Hébert[2], the painter, Director of the Villa Medici, who was in despair at not getting it—for a background to a picture he is painting. Now the Barbaro is ours, there is some fun in beautifying it—and you will see many improvements. Angelo writes that they have just discovered a secret staircase, in the wall, bricked up—behind the small salon. Could this have been for spies? who used to be about the path and bed of all Venetians [. . .].

Ever with love, your affectionate

Ariana

NOTES

1. At Palazzo Barberini in Rome.

2. Antoine Auguste Ernest Hébert (1817–1908), a painter and for many years the director of the French Academy in Rome, Villa Medici (1867–1873, 1885–1891).

V

Ariana Curtis to Mary Curtis
June 6*th* and 7*th* [1887]   Venice, Palazzo Barbaro
(Marciana Ms.)

My dear Mary –

Thanks for your last—telling of the new doctor, and
your change of plan—or rather reverting to your
original one of remaining in Colorado [. . .] The
E.J. Potters have been here—now leaving for Tirol
and Salzkammergut. Dear Mrs. P[otter] is sweet as
ever—but terribly tired and careworn. No maid,
no governess—and tyrannical children. I got her an
Italian girl to come by the day, and relieve her a little—
and I have exhorted her to get a governess. "Mr. Potter
does not like them". The elder girl is an imperious
beauty—the little one, Dolly, a very strange child. They
have brought her here several times, to be left alone in
our Sala, where she talks to herself and recites, and
dreams aloud—that she is a Princess, etc. I should not
encourage such things if she were my child—but they
think it is very interesting. I do not go into the room—
they asked me not to—or rather asked me to let her
come when I was out. Edward has given up singing—
says his children won't let him! However last night, at
my swarry,[1] he was persuaded to, Mlle de Gerstfeld(?)
playing the accompaniment—unluckily the Mocenigo

183

family arrived in the midst, and rather spoiled his effect. (D. calls them *Moce* and other *nigauds*!) I believe Daniel wrote about the wedding of the screaming beauty, Annina Rombo[2], at 9 a.m.! At one time, I thought perhaps she was the coming girl for us—but Ralph did not incline—and it is just as well—for she is, and always will be, surrounded by admirers—which I fancy he would not like in a wife. I begin to think he will not marry—and much regret it[3]. I shall encourage his going over to America soon, in hopes he may see some nice girl there. *Not a word* of any of this, however [. . .] We have had Mr. Symonds here—he is so nice—he is very fond of our garden. Now he has to go back to his prison at Davos—he cannot stay more than a month out of that thin dry air—else he would die—it is a wonder he lives at all. Write how you are feeling and what the Summer climate is.

Ever with love

your

Ariana

NOTES

1. "Soirée", spelt so.

2. Annina Rombo Morosini, a celebrated beauty of the time. In a letter from Bayreuth to Isabella Stewart Gardner, July 23 (1889?), Ralph Curtis wrote that he had painted a portrait of "the exquisite Morosini", "in her loge at the Fenice".

3. Ralph did eventually marry an American on November 3, 1898: the bride was Lisa Colt Rotch (1871–1933), a beautiful young widow and heiress. Of this wedding Henry James wrote to Francis Boott: "Ralph Curtis has just taken to his side a bonnie bride with a nice dead husband and many, I believe, nice living hundreds of thousands" (July 9th 1897). In spite of the fact that Lisa Colt Rotch was in fact a heiress, it was surely a love marriage, as the letters of Ralph Curtis to Bernard Berenson about Lisa clearly show. Lisa's portrait was painted by John Singer Sargent (see letter XXVI) and by Ralph Curtis. See Rosella Mamoli Zorzi, entries for Ralph Curtis, in the catalogue *Venezia. Da Stato a Mito*, Fondazione Cini, Venice, 1997.

VI

Ralph Curtis to Isabella Stewart Gardner
September 18*th* [1889]   Venice, Palazzo Barbaro
(I.S.G.M. Ms)

My dear Mrs. Gardner,
it was quite sweet in you to write me on my birthday.
After hearing the Wagner I wrote you of, I saw
the Dresden gallery and then went to Marienbad
where I had some great sport deer shooting with
the Metternichs whose vast estates are close by. The
Moores[1] and a lot of my friends were taking the cure
there and I passed three most enjoyable weeks. The
music was excellent, climate lovely and the walks well
adapted for my complaint. I have been back 3 weeks.
We have had the Horatios[2] here, and there are the
usual number of agreeable people. Frank Schuster the
great London Wagnerian has taken the Wolkoffs next
Dario[3] charming house all furnished most artistically
for 6 weeks—and has it filled with musical lights and
pretty people. Mrs. Bronson has bought a little scrap
of a house[4] at Asolo to please Mr. Browning who is
now there with them. We miss them awfully. The
Rezzonico is full of "Pen's" friends and his wife's of
course! I have no very recent news of Sargent. The
Moores sailed yesterday for N. Y. to pass 8 weeks to
attend to some money they have recently come into.

Unless Spain[5] carries the day, I shall make a visit this winter, but as I have cried "Wolf. Wolf." so often, of course you won't believe me. Perhaps you are right. My people were never better and join me in the kindest of our regards to you both. Sorry "the orchid's"[6] skin is bad—perhaps that could be remedied by and by! She will be a splendid creature when she is 30 and has had twins. There is a regatta at Murano and from the top of the house I can see the glassy lagoons already speckled with gondolas, so I must hie me there, wishing I had your comely self beside me and could hear your musical mellow voice so suited to confidences by moonlight in Venezia. Such a pity you are wasted out there my dear friend.

Goodbye, ever your affect[ionate]—and cheerful cynic

Ralph Curtis

Did you ever read the fearfully immoral but deeply interesting memoirs of Casanova—of Venice and Europe 150 years ago? 8 vols. But you must get some gnome to buy them for you and then hide them away from eyes and ears of Boston Grandies. Do you know how to make a Venetian blind? You stick your finger in his eye!

NOTES

1. Clara Sophia Jessup Moore (1824–1899) had married Mr. Moore from Philadelphia in 1842. After the death of her husband she moved to England, where she was known for her philanthropic work. She had two daughters, Mary and Ella, of Ralph's age.

2. Horatio F. Brown (1854–1926) and his mother. The English historian lived in Venice for many years, and wrote important books on the history of Venice.

3. Both palaces are on the Grand Canal, near the Salute church.

4. "La Mura", not so small, still the property of Mrs. Bronson's heirs. Mrs. Bronson bought the Asolo house because she had so liked Browning's *Pippa Passes*, set in Asolo.

5. Ralph Curtis painted several "Spanish" subjects: among them *Cigarreras Sevillanas* which was exhibited at the Venice National Exhibition of 1887.

6. Ralph is referring to Margaret Leiter, a friend of Isabella Stewart Gardner, described as "the pretty orchid" in a letter from Bayreuth (July 23). See also letter VII.

VII

Ralph Curtis to Isabella Stewart Gardner
November 20*th* [1888]   Venice, Palazzo Barbaro
(I.S.G.M. Ms.)

My dear Mrs. Gardner,

mea culpa! I have left your letter unanswered for ages. Mea culpa. Do you want a charming apartment[1], next door to Mrs. Bronson in that nice house of the Dutch consul? Your bedroom would be Desdemona's balcony room. You would also have another salon and bedroom on the Grand Canal—charming dining room and guests' room on a very picturesque court and garden—lots of servants' rooms and excellent kitchen. All is in perfect order. 3500 francs a year is asked. The Cyril Flowers (she née Rothschild) nearly took it but his health requires Scotland during vacation. What fun if you should take it, and when you can't come let it to brides and "grooms"on condition that they marry for love.

There will be time for you to answer this here before I go to Florence after Christmas. Then I think of Naples and Palermo, which I don't know. In April I shall take a P. & O. to London stopping over 10 days or so at Seville for the Féria and Old Lang Syne. The spring I shall pass as usual at Paris les Bains. I have not had any news from the MacD.s[2] for ages. They owe me letters, but I owe them so much more! I see Perry Belmont is to replace the excellent Currie. Mrs. Harrison is much improved in health and Peto[3] is to build them a grand house near Henley. John Sargent is in London. He too owes me a letter so I can't give any recent news.

Mrs. George Batten[4] fascinated all the men here during 2 months. Mrs. Moore is now passing a week at the Stanleys' house in London. They are coming to Italy in Jan[uar]y. I went to see them at Ischl after she had done her Marienbad cure. It is a lovely place and I enjoyed my tour in the Tyrol immensely. She is said to have never looked better than now, so taking care of herself all summer was a success.

I am an uncle! Osborne's wife had a baby boy[5] the other day. Laurence will tell you all about his visit to their county and his experiences. Edith Bronson enjoyed her summer in USA and looks much improved by it. Poor Mrs. B[ronson] I don't think looks very well in spite of (yet perhaps because of) the 10 weeks of visit of R. Browning and his sister to their tiny house, which she thinks must be filled day and night with people to make the lion roar. By the way you are sure to know Miss Amelie Reeves[6], as was, so tell her that Browning after hearing the fuss over her "Quick or the Dead" read it, saw *nothing* improper in it, except some very bad English here and there, and found it "very strong and original, especially the scene with the parson—a touch of genius in that story and a great promise for the future. I should like to have passed the A.M. in going over the MMS. and changing the few things which would have made it truly a remarkable piece of work". It would be kind to let her know of his applause, so please do so. The Howes are still here, buoyant as ever. They go soon to Rome. I have been staying with the Morosinis, Rombos, Pisanis and Marcellos at the villas, which are far more civilized than I had supposed and their society is queer and amusing to study. Lawn tennis has just reached them—and some drive 4 in hands and all have 5 o'clock teas and bonbons from Boissière—"Juge un peu" as they say in Marseilles. A French governess read out the story of Susanna and the Elders to the Contessina Amalia aged 15—"Voilà, Mademoiselle, une conduite digne d'éloges." Amalia after a moment's reflection "Oui, mais elle aurait peut être aussi bien fait d'en prendre *le moins vieux*"! Where is Miss Leiter and have you had the Spanish Cotillon[7] yet? I shan't be able to get to America till . . . till . . . next year.

Can't you run over to see the Paris Exp[osition] if there is no war. I am going to Bayreuth if they give Tristan. With kindest regards to Mr. Gardner and regrets that they would let me do the Carpaccios (so

I owe you several francs) I remain dear Mrs. Gardner your ever affectionate friend

Ralph Curtis

Henry James driven to death by the printer's devil (what a pity he knows no other) has returned to London via Paris. He is to stay at the Barbaro again in April.

I have been twice to stir up Carrer about your piece of furniture. The carving and joining is nearly done and very satisfact[or]y indeed.

NOTES

1. The Gothic Palazzetto Contarini Fasan, called "Desdemona's House", on the Grand Canal, across from the Salute church.

2. Perhaps the McDoughals, friends of the Curtises.

3. Harold Peto, the English architect. He was the son of Sir Samuel Morton Peto. Born in 1854, went to Harrow and studied architecture. After working with the architectural firm of Ernest George until 1892 in England, he worked on his own on the continent and designed three villas in the Italian Renaissance style, on the Côte d'Azur between 1902 and 1910. One of the villas was Ralph Curtis's Villa Sylvia. On these villas see Graeme Moore, "Renaissance d'Azur", in *Country Life*, July 7, 1988, pp.156–158 (with photos). Ralph Curtis described to Isabella Stewart Gardner the interior of the villa, which had a loggia and a wonderful garden: "The dining room is white wood and Chippendale. The big sala ivory white and chestnut doors and wainscoating (sic) and a cinquecento black fireplace from Viterbo, very big".

4. Née Mabel Hatch. Sargent painted her portrait.

5. Henry Osborne Curtis (1888–1964), the son of Osborne, Ralph's younger brother.

6. Amélie Rives (not Reeves) (1863–1945), later known as Princess Troubetzkoy, published the novel *The Quick or the Dead?* in *Lippincott Magazine* in 1888. It told the story of a young widow's love for her dead husband's cousin, who looked very much like the husband, and her giving up her love. The novel was a great success and caused some turmoil because the descriptions of the relationships between the two characters were considered too realistic and risqué.

7. Spanish cotillons were described by Ralph as follows: "These cotillons favours are embroidered in silk, gold, and silver by the ladies, 'God bless them', of Seville, and the day before the fight are paraded through the streets with a band of Estudiantina guitars, and *are pinned onto a huge cross*!" (Letter to Isabella Stewart Gardner).

VIII

Ralph Curtis to Isabella Stewart Gardner
May 25*th* [1896]   Venice, Palazzo Barbaro
(I.S.G.M.Ts.)

Dear Queen Isabella –

I got your word "BUYVO"[1]—so I took "VO" to mean
that you would *also* like a most splendid *piviale*[2] which
Richetti also had—crimson velvet on a cream *fond*—
like the small piece you so admired in our red room,
on the door to the left of the little Flemish Madonna.
I beat Satan down to letting you have the fire dogs and
this textile gem for *2000* lire—1600 lire for the fire
irons[3]—400 for the *piviale*, which you can send him a
cheque for at your convenience. I can safely assure you
that they are both admirable acquisitions.

My people's Indian guests have just gone. The
Rodds[4] arrive anon to stay with us. Lady Kenmare[5]
is here and hosts and hosts of USAers are in all the
hotels. Bode[6] of Berlin Museum—Yriarte[7]—the
Monacos—Lady Airlie—Sybil Sanderson (who had all
her jewels stolen on the train from her trunks)—Mrs.
Gilder—the Tom Perrys[8]—Wa(l)ter Gays[9]—Frank
Lathrop[10] the painter—Marcuard[11] the Florence
connaisseur, are among the fine flowers which bloom
tra-la-la. Nevertheless I am off soon to Paris, having
about finished my big picture, which has turned out

194

really quite good. I am waiting for gold coins from our copper.

Do write me a good letter, and another when these things reach you—and with most cordial alibayons to you both—I remain

ever your affec[tionate]ly

"Redman" gnome.

P.S. Pen is made a cavaliere del Regno. Lady Hally has been presented by England with a house at Asolo! H.R.H handed her the deed with a merry Xmas! Pen furious!!

NOTES

1. Isabella Stewart Gardner would telegraph with a code system her approval or refusal to her various art providers, among whom, as is well known, the most important was Bernard Berenson.

2. "*Piviale*", i.e. pluvial (ceremonial vestment).

3. "In the tapestry room" is added on the side.

4. Sir James Rennell Rodd (1858–1941), diplomatist, poet, and author of *Social and Diplomatic Memories 1884–1893*. A friend of Ralph Curtis, he spent his honeymoon in Venice, staying at Palazzo Barbaro (1895). He was ambassador in Rome in 1891–92, where he saw ecclesiastics, artists, and such intellectuals as J. A. Symonds, G. Boni, the excavator of the Forum, Axel Muenthe, Paul Bourget, Count Primoli. He was also a friend

of the Storys.

5. Gertrude-Harriet Thynne (1840–1913) had married Valentine Augustus (Browne) Lord Kenmare (1825–1903), of Killarney, County Kerry, Ireland, in 1858. Lady Kenmare was a very close friend of Ariana, and spent some time every year in Palazzo Barbaro. On the two ladies' friendship see Henry James, *Letters to Miss Allen*, cit.

6. Wilhelm von Bode, the Director of the Karl-Friedrich Museum in Berlin, and the author of *Mein Leben* (reprinted by Nicholaische Verlag in 1997, in two volumes).

7. Charles Yriarte (1833–1898), writer and director of the *Monde illustré*. He wrote several works concerning Italy, among which *Venise* (1877), *Veronese* (1888), *Fortuny* (1886), *La vie d'un patricien de Venise* (1874).

8. Thomas Sargent Perry (1845–1928), American author and scholar, taught at Harvard, and married the painter Lila Cabot in 1874. He was a friend of Henry James who wrote about him in *Notes of a Son and Brother.*

9. Walter Gay (1856–1937), an American painter. His pictures of interiors represent halls and rooms strictly without people.

10. Francis Lathrop (1849–1909), an American painter who studied in London.

11. Friedrich von Marcuard (1845–1917), the Swiss painter, art historian and collector, the author of *Die Zeichnungen Michelangelos* (1901). He lived in Florence from 1871 onwards.

IX

Ralph Curtis to Isabella Stewart Gardner
20*th* May 1911   Venice, Palazzo Barbaro
(I.S.G.M. Ms.)

My dear Queen –

Why do you never send me anything but a post card
in 6 months? I came here from Villa Sylvia 10 days
ago, and now go to Paris to help feather our nest
there, 40 ave[nue] Trocadero (pin *that* to your hat).
I am so sorry to have just missed Laura Wagnière
who was a fortnight with mama. The Campanile
grows[1]—the place is full—and today there is a
grand scheme to have a sub-mud electric tram to the
Lido!!! Mama, except for stiff knees, is very fit, and
is agog to go as near as she can to the Coronation[2].
Sargent has just been to Paris to see the Ingres show.
I hear Gay's picture of the "Barbarian's Palace"[3] is
to go to the Boston Museum. I wish I had time to
go to stay with B.B.[4] who is giving brain banquets
at "I Tatti". Mrs. Mary is still at Oxford, after the
death of her mother, who talks affec[tionate]ly of
you. I am so glad he is better. What of your plan of
coming abroad? There is lots to see, hear and feel,
but precious little to buy, unless one is from Pittsburg,
and a damn fool, too. I expect to read of you in the

grand stand waving a banner at the internat[ional] polo match. Nevertheless I persist in remaining your affec[ionate]

Raffaello

NOTES

1. The Campanile of St. Mark's had fallen in 1902 and it was being rebuilt.

2. The coronation of George V in England.

3. The title of the painting is *The Barbaro Palace*. It represented the grand ballroom of the Barbaro, strictly without human figures. It is now at the Boston Museum of Fine Arts. See W. Gay, *op.cit.*, n.15.

4. Bernhard Berenson (later Bernard) (1865–1959), the famous art historian, and his wife Mary Pearsall Smith (1864–1945). Berenson settled in Florence in 1889, and rented I Tatti in 1900, the year he married Mary. Ralph Curtis had great affection for Bernard Berenson, as his letters to B.B. testify.

X

Ralph Curtis to Isabella Stewart Gardner
May 17*th* [1914]   Venice, Palazzo Barbaro
(I.S.G.M. Ms.)

Eccomi, carissima Regina[1], nothing much new, except
the campanile[2] and the bric-à-brac. My mother is
just the same, the old house quite as you recall it.
Even Mancini[3] is coming to see me this afternoon.
[. . .] Mrs. Eden has broken her leg and will be lame
for life. He is handsomer than ever, a Padre Eterno!
The exhibition is odious[4]. There is no good taste left,
outside pastrycook's.

From here I go to B.B.s. In Paris he gave himself
the most expensive object he ever bought, a Chinese
scroll of exquisite beauty, and he is now absorbed in
Tang poetry![5] Russell's[6] company is "making good" in
Paris. Smart Parisians will never make it popular with
their set, but the few who love music and foreigners
will make it pay . . . apparently. Dumas told our
national Emma[7]: "En France nous aimons la musique
militaire et les Chansonnettes". John's picture of
James[8] can be repaired and will get the Victoria cross
for distinguished service. Henry now looks like a
kind Cardinal, doesn't he. Every hotel and lodging
in Venice is full. As soon as it gets warmer beds will
be put in gondolas. Morton Prince[9] and our national

Edith are now at "I Tatti". How serious a savant do you take him to be? Goodbye my dear.
Ever your affectionate slave
Raffaello*

* a good deal better

NOTES

1. "Here I am, very dear Queen."

2. The new campanile was inaugurated in 1912.

3. Antonio Mancini (1852–1930), an artist who painted the portraits of the Curtises and of Isabella Stewart Gardner among others.

4. The eleventh "Esposizione Internazionale d'Arte della città di Venezia" for 1914. Ralph Curtis had exhibited his own

paintings in the second International Exhibition of Venice, in 1897, and previously in the annual National Exhibition (1887). He had also participated in the Paris Exposition Universelle of 1889. By 1914 Ralph had given up painting. His decision to do so was the "germ" of one story by Edith Wharton, "The Verdict" (1908), where a painter suddenly realizes his art is no good as compared to the real art of a great painter. The story caused a turmoil in the Curtis circle, shocking especially Lisa, in spite of Henry Adams's efforts to explain the whole thing.

5. Berenson bought a number of beautiful Chinese scrolls and oriental art pieces, especially between 1910 and 1917; see L.P. Roberts, "Preface", p.8, *The Bernard Berenson Collection of Oriental Art at Villa I Tatti*, New York, Hudson Hills Press, 1991.

6. Henry Russell's Boston opera, which was touring Europe.

7. "Our national Emma" is Emma Eames (1865–1952), a famous American opera singer, the wife of Julian Russell Story (1867–1919), son of William Wetmore Story.

8. Sargent's portrait of Henry James, done on the latter's seventieth birthday, was vandalised with a meat-cleaver by a Suffragette at the Royal Academy in 1914. The protest was not against either the painter or the subject, but to demonstrate that there was "no security" for property or art treasures "until women are given their political freedom" (Edel, *The Master*, p.490).

9. Morton Prince (1854–1929), the American psychologist and neurologist, author of important studies, among which *The Dissociation of Personality* (1906). Edith is Edith Wharton (1862–1937), the American writer, and a friend of the Berensons and Henry James.

XI

Ralph Curtis to Isabella Stewart Gardner
2*nd* September [1915]   Venice, Palazzo Barbaro
(I.S.G.M.Ts.)

Dear Queen,
Here I am again, in the dear old place with which
I always connect *you*. I find my mother hardly at
all changed. She is bomb-proof as to nerves. The
servants are in such a funk that she feels it would be
mean to leave them in their fright. So she refuses to
go away. I in vain tell her it isn't *good* for her nerves.
The mosquitos from Pola come buzzing over nearly
every fine night, and drop bombs for half an hour
or so[1]. So far the damage has not been great, but
any time irreparable disaster may happen. I shall
stay a fortnight. Venice is like a lovely prima donna
in deep mourning. All the gilded angels wear sackcloth painted dirty grey. Anything that shines is
covered. At night all is as black as in the dark ages.
"Serrenos"[2] call out "all is well" every half hour. But
when danger is signalled the elec[tric] light is cut off,
sirens blow, cannon firebombs explode and the whole
city shakes on its piles. All the hotels but the Danieli's
are hospitals. No antiquaire is open. The only
foreigners are those who own places here. Nobody is
allowed to paint or photograph. At night the waiters

at Florian's give change with pocket electric lamps for a moment on the table. Many more have been drowned by tumbling into the black canals than have been killed by the enemy. Posts and bars are put up at all dangerous corners. San Marco is a fortress of sand bags [. . .] We are so exhilarated by the good news from all the fronts. At last the beginning of the end seems in sight, but we expect still another winter of it, and possibly 18 months. Mama joins in best love to you, dear Queen. Ever yours affectionate

Raffaello

NOTES

1. For the photographic representation of Venice's war defenses (including sand bags, etc.) see G. Scarabello, *Il martirio di Venezia durante la Grande Guerra*, Venezia, Tipografia del Gazzettino, 1933. The book also has a list of aerial incursions. The envelope of this letter carries the war stamp *verificato per censura* (i.e. verified by censors).

2. A possible mistake of Ralph Curtis, who seems to be using the Spanish word *sereno*. In a letter to Isabella Stewart Gardner from Seville he writes: "the Sereno, with his halberd and lantern, passes under my balcony, crying 'Ave Maria purissima—*las doce y sereno*' ".

The Ballroom, Palazzo Barbaro

NOTES BY ARIANA CURTIS

(Marciana Ms.)

Many interesting people have been at Pal[azzo] Barbaro during our time. The most so was Robert Browning who constantly dined here, during his many visits to Venice—and whose doings and sayings D.S.C. recorded[1]. Then a frequent guest was J.A. Symonds[2]—a delightful companion—and dear Henry James—who often stayed with us. John Sargent[3] has very often been a visitor—always most welcome—and many lesser artists from "Carolus" Duran[4] down came here when Ralph lived with us. Empress F[rederic]k[5] came to tea three or four times with her daughter. Also the present Queen of Sweden[6]—then Crown Princess—Princess Christian[7], and her daughter—and Princess Charlotte of Meiningen[8], all interesting to me as children and grandchildren of the beloved Louisa[9].

I have since regretted that I never kept a visitors' book. The most beloved guest was Gertrude Countess of Kenmare[10] who for nine happy years passed always three or four weeks in May or June with us—and whose loving friendship has been one of the great joys of my life.

General de Horsey[11] has always been an habitué of the Barbaro—and is full of most interesting recollections of old Venice in the Austrian days.

And the society of our faithful friend and neighbour Horatio Brown[12] has always been a great pleasure to us both.

I hope to revise and enlarge these notes, hurriedly written at R.W.C.'s request—when we return from England—and I have ordered a copy made of Fontana's detailed description of the Palace[13].

The arcade was in terrible condition. I took R[ichar]d Hunt[14], the American architect to see it, and told him our plans for restoring it. He said "you will never make anything of it" which was a douche of cold water.

However we persevered, and made it what it now is. We would have liked to reopen the arches—but it was unsafe to do so—and they would have had to be filled with iron grilles to keep thieves out, which would have added weight, without support. So we rebuilt the wall, so as to show the columns, just in six old quattrocento windows corresponding to those in the façade—but two columns at the entrance from the cortile, with capitals which come from Ca'd'Oro, and had been replaced there by copies, made by Biondetti! (see *Stones of Venice*.) Biondetti had these capitals and many other Grecian fragments in his San Vio marble-yard at that time,—also a large capital of Pentelic marble, which had been removed from San Marco or the Doge's Palace. We had the centre sawed out, with a circular saw, and set it up as a well head in the cortile,—the original one having been removed before our day. We were sure there must be a pointed arch on the G[ran]d Canal, and it was quite exciting when the plaster and bricks above the low modern door were knocked away, to see the ogive peak reappear. The arch was all there—but the ornamental part was gone. We found some old pilasters, however, and then the question came of how to fill the top. At last D.S.C. thought of having the design of the beautiful balcony of the so-called "Casa di Desdemona" copied in iron—which was done well by Bellotto—a poor blacksmith, with the soul of a cinquecento artist, who literally danced for joy when we gave him beautiful designs to execute—such as the above and the gate of the Abbaye of Fécamp, in Normandy, which he made for our Cortile. He was a poet too—but died young, unhappily—leaving a son who is a worthy successor.

We found a great deal to do in the great drawing-room. A beam below the "clerestory" windows had nearly rotted away, from rain having filtered in, and had to be replaced.

The wings and feet of many of the stucco putti were broken—apparently children had been allowed to throw hard balls at them, as we found several such on the cornice! Then Mrs. Ker[15] had covered the ceiling pictures with bitumen! saying she did not like faces looking down at her!! We had a great scaffolding built, and cleaned the pictures, which were so confused one could not tell what they represented. The centre one, which we had thought might be the Deluge, turned out to be a Roman Triumph, with Zenobia in front of the Conqueror's Car—her hands tied with pearl ropes! and the four others seem to be the Sibyls— one on horseback. *The three mural decorations are Mutius Scevola by Piazzetta, Sabines Luca Giordano, Darius's family before Alex[ander] by Pontebasso. The stucchi 1650, botega di A. Vittoria*[16].

26 June 1908

NOTES

1. D. S. Curtis's "Diary", now at the Biblioteca Nazionale Marciana, under press. On the subject see, Rosella Mamoli Zorzi, "A Venetian Diary" cit.

2. See note 2 to James's letter XVIII.

3. See notes 3 and 4 to James's letter XXVI.

4. Carolus-Duran (1837–1917), the French painter, also the teacher of Ralph Curtis in Paris.

5. Empress Frederick, née Victoria, Princess Royal of England (1840–1901), daughter of Queen Victoria. She married Frederick of Prussia (1831–1888) in 1858. Frederick became the emperor on the death of William I, in 1888, and reigned for 98 days.

6. Sophie of Nassau, the wife of Oscar III of Sweden.

7. Louisa, the wife of Christian, Crown Prince of Denmark.

8. Charlotte von Meiningen, née Princess of Prussia (1860), married Bernard, the Duke of Saxe-Meiningen in 1878.

9. Louisa, née Princess of the Netherlands (1828–1871), married Charles X of Sweden (1826–1873), the mother of Princess Louisa of Denmark.

10. See note 5 to Ralph Curtis's Letter VIII.

11. General de Horsey lived in the Palazzo Semitecolo, near the Salute, on the Grand Canal. Constance Woolson committed suicide from that building.

12. See note 2 to Ralph Curtis's Letter VI.

13. The volume G.J. Fontana, *Cento palazzi di Venezia storicamente illustrati* published in 1850.

14. Richard Morris Hunt (1827–1895), the American architect, well known above all for the Newport mansions (e.g. Vanderbilt House).

15. Olga (Nini) Kerr, a British lady whose brother Gervase lived in Venice. She was a friend of Mrs. Bronson.

16. The lines printed here in italics were added in pencil, in a different hand. Pontebasso is Fontebasso. "*The Roman Triumph, with Zenobia . . .*" is the central painting of the grand salon, by Antonio Zanchi, the artist of the other four paintings on the ceiling, *Ipsicrateia Cutting her Hair to Wear a Helmet, Queen Artemisia Drinking the Ashes of her Deceased Husband, Clelia Delivered to King Porsenna, Ersilia Witnessing the Duel.* Scholars agree on the subjects, but not quite on the dates (from 1690 to the first decade of the eighteenth century). On the subject see, I. Chiappini di Sorio, "Decorazioni del soffitto di Palazzo Barbaro", in *I pittori bergamaschi dal XIII al XIX secolo. Il Seicento*, Bergamo, Poligrafiche Bolis, 1987, pp.577–579. On Zanchi see "Antonio Zanchi" by P. Zampetti, in the same volume. On the ceiling paintings see also B. Hanemann, "Antonio Zanchi and the ceiling of the Salone of the Palazzo Barbaro Curtis", in *Arte Veneta*, XXXVII, 1983, pp.201–205. See also A. Riccoboni, "Antonio Zanchi e la pittura veneziana del Seicento", in *Saggi e memorie di storia dell'arte*, V, 1966, pp.53–135. The *Mutius Scevola* is by Piazzetta, the *Sabines* (here attributed to Luca Giordano) is by Sebastiano Ricci, *Darius's Family*, here attributed to Fontebasso, is instead *Coriolanus* by Balestra. On Piazzetta see *L'opera completa del Piazzetta*, Preface by R. Pallucchini, ed. by A. Mariuz, Milan, Rizzoli, 1982. On Fontebasso, see M. Magrini, *Francesco Fontebasso*, Vicenza, Neri Pozza, 1988; on S. Ricci, see J. Daniels, *Sebastiano Ricci*, Wayland Publ., 1976. The stuccowork does not

seem to be the work of Vittoria, but the work of Ticino artists of the mid-XVIII century. On the *stucco* works and paintings of the salon see B J. K. Aikema, "Le decorazioni di Palazzo Barbaro-Curtis a Venezia fino a metà del Settecento", in *Arte Veneta*, XLI, 1987, pp.147–153. For the Tiepolo ovals that were sold between 1866 and 1874 see F. Pedrocco, M. Gemin, *Giambattista Tiepolo*, Venezia, Arsenate, 1993, pp.408–409, A. Bayer, "Le decorazioni per Ca' Barbaro", in *1696–1996 Giambattista Tiepolo*, Milano, Skira, 1996, pp.157–166, and the essay by D. De Grazia in D. De Grazia, E. Garbeson et al., in *Italian Paintings of the XVII and XVIII Century*, Washington, National Gallery of Art, 1996, pp.265–272.

The Courtyard, Palazzo Barbaro

NOTES BY PATRICIA CURTIS VIGANÒ

I have been asked to write a few lines about my home, Palazzo Barbaro. It is difficult to know where to begin. Why not start by saying that it has been part of my life from the day I first walked up the beautiful staircase that leads to the *piano nobile*.

I have vague recollections of arriving by gondola, the same gondola that today stands majestically in the courtyard in spite of it being out of its natural habitat. It was dark and mysterious, and as we stepped into the courtyard and approached what to me seemed the steepest staircase I had ever seen, my father took my hand. I was four years old.

I was not in the least intimidated by the immensity of the Barbaro, which, at the time, was entirely open and counted sixty-one rooms, lights blazing. It was all very much to my liking and became intensely more so as the years went by. I have always felt I belonged here and much happiness has this extraordinary palace given me.

Henry James believed that the Barbaro had moods. I can assure the reader that it does.

As I write these lines in the cool silence of a sunlit

afternoon, innumerable memories cross my mind, all dominated by the spirit of the Barbaro and by that touch of magic that has always enchanted me as it does this moment, looking up and wondering at the beauty and harmony of it all.

How unfortunate that these walls cannot speak! They love to be loved and, in return, they have given inspiration to artists, writers and poets. Perhaps what moves today's sensitive visitor is the unchanged elegance and serene atmosphere of decorative perfection.

There is, however, something else, the soul, that is what Henry James felt, and of which he wrote.

I recall a particularly pleasant and fascinating afternoon in the library, honoured by the visit of the great Jamesian scholar, Leon Edel and of his wife in 1984. All sorts of extraordinary persons have come again and again, happy to return to Venice, the unique and most beautiful city, and anxious to revisit the Barbaro.

At the end of the last century the Barbaro was most certainly an intellectual Salon at its peak. Very often an invitation to tea also meant listening to Robert Browning read some of his work, while on the upper floor Sargent and my grandfather Ralph spent the afternoon painting in the large studio facing north, towards the courtyard and Santo Stefano.

Claude Monet, much to his regret, came to Venice only once, in 1908. He was a guest of my great-grandparents, Daniel and Ariana Curtis. He spent most of his time painting from our Watergate. It must have been wonderfully peaceful in those days, with no *serenate* and no motorboats to interrupt his *coup de pinceau* as he painted Palazzo Polignac, which faces us across the Grand Canal.

In the 1950s I vividly remember Serge Lifar joyfully walking into the Ballroom as he did every year at precisely six in the afternoon, on August 18th. There was no need to confirm the invitation. We knew that arriving in Venice his wish was to visit the Barbaro and its inhabitants, and that the next day, August 19th, he would, unfailingly, go to the island of San Michele and lay a rose on Diaghilev's tomb. He could be anywhere in the world but, from wherever he was, he would return to Venice and lay the rose, until the year he died.

In the same decade the Barbaro walls witnessed a somewhat frivolous moment when my parents decided to give a ball in honour of Brigitte Bardot. I will never forget my astonishment at seeing Harry Belafonte striding alone through the *portego* singing "Matilda"!

A few years ago, a most gracious Queen Beatrix of the Netherlands requested a private visit accompanied by her husband, Prince Claus, and a few friends. She visited the *piano nobile*, then drifted up to the library where Her Majesty instantly decided to forget all time-tables and sat on a not so comfortable armchair. We enjoyed the candle-lit library while several bodyguards were pacing the floor of the entrance hall.

Another wonderful friend of the Barbaro was the painter Giuseppe Santomaso, whose first words of greeting upon arrival were "Patricia, your extravagant *folly* is still part of you, is it not? Please answer yes." I would smile, which meant that, yes, I was happily struggling to keep the atmosphere intact and the walls content.

There have been multitudes of friends, and friends of friends, that during my lifetime have warmed these marble halls with their interest and their encouragement in not allowing the "soul" to escape.

I thank them all.

May 1997

ABBREVIATIONS OF LETTER HEADINGS:

Edel I, II, III, IV	*The Letters of Henry James*, ed. by Leon Edel, The Belknap Press of Harvard University Press, volumes 1–4, 1974–1984.
I.S.G.M. MS. and TS.	Isabella Stewart Gardner Museum, Manuscript and Typescript.
Dartmouth MS. and TS.	The Dartmouth College Library, Manuscript and Typescript.
Marciana MS.	The Biblioteca Nazionale Marciana, Manuscript (Venice).

The main sources for the notes of this book are: the four volumes of *The Letters of Henry James*, ed. by Leon Edel, The Belknap Press of Harvard University Press, 1974–1984, and the five volumes of Edel's biography of Henry James (Discus Books); *The Complete Notebooks of Henry James*, ed. by Leon Edel and H.L. Powers, Oxford University Press, 1987; Henry James and Edith Wharton, *Letters 1905–1915*, ed. by L. H. Powers, London, Weidenfeld and Nicolson, 1990; Edith Wharton, *A Backward Glance*, New York, Scribner's, 1984; R. W. B. Lewis, *Edith Wharton. A Biography*, New York, Fromm, 1985; *The Letters of Bernard Berenson and Isabella Stewart Gardner*, ed. by Rollin N. van Hadley, Boston, Northeastern University Press, 1987; *More than Friend, The Letters of Robert Browning to Katherine de Kay Bronson*, ed. by Michael Meredith, Armstrong Browning Library and Wedgestone Press, 1985; Regina Soria, *The Dictionary of 19th Century American Artists in Italy*, Farleigh Dickinson University Press, 1982; Henry James, *Lettere da Palazzo Barbaro*, and *Letters to Miss Allen*, edited by Rosella Mamoli Zorzi, Milano, Archinto, 1989 and 1993.

INDEX

Adams, Henry 201
Airlie, Lady 194
Albrizzi, palazzo 22
Aldrich, Thomas Bailey 97
Alford, Lady 23
Allen, Jessie 42, 47, 167, 169
Alvarez, Eugenio 182
Alvisi, casa or palazzino 28, 73, 77, 81, 85, 91, 144
Angelo (Sitran) 20, 115, 116, 129, 168, 178, 182

Baldwin, William Wilberforce 105, 106, 112, 118, 140
Balestra, Antonio 22
Barbaro, Almorò 21, 48
Barbaro, Antonio 22, 49
Barbaro, Daniele 21, 36, 48
Barbaro, Francesco 21, 48, 49
Barbaro, Marc'Antonio (+1858) 180
Barbaro, Marc'Antonio, 22, 48, 49
Barbaro, Zaccaria, 21, 48
Barbesi, casa 28, 57, 71
Bardot, Brigitte 215
Basso, Elisa 180
Batten, Mabel 190, 193
Beatrix, Queen of the Netherlands 216
Belafonte, Harry 216
Bellini, Gentile 43
Bellini, Giovanni 60, 62, 63, 72
Benson, Eugene 160, 165, 166
Berenson, Bernard 185, 195, 197, 198, 199, 201
Berenson Pearsall Smith, Mary 197, 198

Biondetti, casa 19, 52, 143, 145, 146
Blumenthal, Jakob 176
Bode, Wilhelm von 194, 196
Boni, Giacomo 196
Bonifazio (de Pitati), 69
Boott, Francis 42, 91, 93, 137, 139, 185
Boott, Lizzie 42, 93, 138, 139
Bordone, Paris 69
Bourbon, don Carlos de 81, 84
Bourget, Paul 94, 154, 196
Brichieri, villa 29, 94, 100
Bronson, Arthur 66, 73
Bronson de Kay, Katherine 14, 28, 29, 30, 40, 44, 52, 53, 66, 73, 76, 80,81,87,92, 116, 117, 120, 122, 129, 132, 140, 143, 144, 146, 153, 157, 172, 175, 176, 186, 188, 189, 190, 210
Bronson Rucellai Edith 73, 116, 122, 140, 146, 190
Brooke, Lady (Ranee of Sarawak) 125, 127, 149, 154
Brooke, Sir James 127
Brown, Horatio 14, 186, 206
Browning Fannie v. Coddington, Fannie
Browning, "Pen" (Robert Wiedemann) 81, 84, 104, 129, 138, 186, 195
Browning, Robert 14, 40, 41, 44, 53, 73,"81, 84, 92, 172, 176, 179, 190, 205
Browning, Sarianna 172, 176, 179, 190
Bulwer-Lytton, Edward 88, 90
Byron, Lord 38, 83

Caliari, Carlo 69
Cantoni, Israele 180
Cantoni, Sofia 180
Cappello, palazzo (Grand Canal) 44
Cappello, palazzo (Rio Marin) 160, 161, 162, 166
Carpaccio, Vittore 69
Carrer 40, 122, 123, 192
Carriera, Rosalba 19, 145
Carter, Grace 140, 142
Casanova, Giacomo 187
Clairmont, Claire 52
Claus, Prince Consort, 216
Clerlé, Anselmo 180
Coburn, Alvin Langdon 35, 36, 160, 165, 166
Coddington, Fannie 84, 132
Constable, John 152, 153
Contarini Corfù, palazzo 84
Contarini dagli Scrigni, palazzo, 84
Contarini dal Zaffo, palazzo, 19, 81
Contarini Fasan, palazzetto 189, 192
Cooper, James Fenimore 29, 38, 52, 174
Cornaro, Caterina 88, 90
Cotman. John S, 152, 153
Crawshay, Robert Thompson 179, 180
Curtis Lisa 16, 156, 157, 159, 185, 201
Curtis, Mary 46, 171, 174, 175, 178, 181, 183
Curtis, Osborne 90, 148, 150, 175, 190, 193
Curtis, Ralph, 16, 17, 24, 25, 46, 47, 48, 54, 90, 129, 185, 187, 188, 189, 192–203, 206, 209

Da Mula, palazzo 19
Dante Alighieri 72, 83, 118
Dario, palazzo 19, 138, 186
Delacroix, Eugène 63
Diaghilev, Sergej 215
Disraeli, Benjamin 88, 90

Dodge, Mabel 166
Domenico (D'Este) 20, 125, 126, 171
Doré, Gustave 60, 72
Duran, Carolus 159, 205, 209
Duveneck, Franck 42, 44, 93, 139, 172, 175, 176

Eames, Emma 199, 201
Eden, Frederic and Caroline 116, 117, 120, 122
Ehrenfreund, Alberto 180
Elisa 115, 120

Fiske, Willard 80, 83
Fletcher, Constance 52, 160, 164, 165, 166
Flower, Cyril 189
Fontebasso, Francesco 210
Foscari, palazzo 128, 130
Franchetti, palazzo 163
Frederick III, Emperor of Germany 209
Frederick, Empress 17, 205, 209
Fuller, Margaret 139
Furnivall, F.J. 180

Gamba, Countess 37, 80
Gamba, Guiccioli Teresa 37, 80, 83
Gardner, Isabella Stewart 13, 15, 16, 24, 26, 30, 31, 40, 41, 47, 50, 51, 53, 54, 74, 76, 101, 107, 109, 114, 121, 122, 123, 124, 129, 146, 185, 186, 188, 189, 192–197, 199, 202, 203
Gardner, John Lowell 122, 125, 126, 192
Gaspari, Antonio 22
Gatterburg Morosini, Loredana 177
Gautier, Théophile 61, 66, 72, 73
Gay, Walter 24, 50, 194, 196, 197, 198
Giordano, Luca 208, 210
Giusti, Giuseppe 80
Giustinian Recanati, palazzo 81, 92

Gordon, Sir Alexander 176
Greenough, Horatio 93, 174
Greenough, Laura 174
Greenough, Sara 173, 174, 177
Guggenheim, Peggy, Collection v.
    Venier dei Leoni

Hamilton, Eugene Lee 79, 83
Hardy, Thomas 136
Hébert, Antoine Auguste 182
Hickey, Emily 180
Hildebrand, Adolf von 80, 83
Hohenlohe family 143
Holas, Maria 142
Holford, Mrs. 122
Horsey, General de 138, 206, 209
Howells, William Dean 57, 71
Huebner, Baron 176
Hulton, Zina 31, 51
Hunt, Richard Morris 206, 210
Huntington, Henry 92
Huntington, Mrs. 117, 120
Hurtado family 81

Incontri, Marchesa 78, 79

Jack, Mrs., v. Gardner, Isabella
    Stewart
James Henry Sr. (father) 139
James, Alice (Henry's sister) 42, 83,
    103
James, Alice (William's wife) 127
James, William 42, 57, 71, 83, 125,
    127, 133
Jenna, Isacco 180
Johnson-Brooke, Charles Anthony
    127

Kemble, Fanny 90
Kenmare, Lady Gertrude-Harriet
    194, 196, 205
Kenmare, Lord 196
Ker, Miss 172
Ker, Olga 208, 210

LaFarge, John 33, 51, 57, 71
Lathrop, Frank 194, 196
Latimer, Ralph 25, 50
Layard, Lady Enyd 43, 81, 84
Layard, Sir Austen 43, 81, 84
Leiter, Margaret 188
Lifar, Serge 215
Loredan, palazzo 19, 84
Louisa, Princess of Denmark 205, 209
Louisa, Queen of Sweden 205, 209
Lovelace, Lord 166
Lowell, Johnny 172, 174
Lowell, Percival 174
Ludovisi, villa 86
Lyall, Barbara 173, 176

Mancini, Antonio 199, 200
Mantegna, Andrea 41
Marcello family 191
Marcuard, Friedrich von 194, 196
Marsh, George Perkins 80, 84
McClellan family 96
Meiningen, Charlotte von 205, 209
Meissonnier, Jean-Louis-Ernest 174
Metternich, Prince Paul and Princess
    Mélanie 81, 84, 186
Mocenigo family 81, 84, 184
Mocenigo, Laura 44, 172
Monet, Claude 215
Montalba family 116, 120
Montecuccoli, Count 84
Montenegro, King of 40
Montenegro, Princess Olga of 40
Montenegro, Queen Darinka of
    40, 43
Moore family 186, 188, 190
Morelli, Giovanni 43, 53
Morosini, Annina v. Rombo
Morosini family 191
Morosini, Francesco 22
Morosini, palazzo 176, 177
Muenthe, Axel 196
Mundella, Anthony 176, 177
Musatti, Cesare 23, 180, 200, 202,
    203

Nash, Thomas 38
Nassau, Sophie of 205, 209
Norton, Charles Eliot 83
Norton, Grace 25, 42, 77, 83, 98, 110, 114

Oliphant, Laurence 174
Ombrellino, villa 100

Paget, Violet 79, 83
Palladio, Andrea 21, 22
Palma II Giovane and Palma il Vecchio 69
Peabody Russell, Mr. 84
Perrault, Charles 72
Perry, Thomas Sargent 194, 196
Peruzzi Story, Edith 105, 106, 113, 119
Peruzzi, Ubaldo 106
Peto, Harold 190, 193
Petrarch, Francesco 80, 83
Piazzetta, Gian Battista 22, 208, 210
Pilat, Mme de 176
Pisani, Almorò 89, 90, 149, 150
Pisani family 191
Pisani van Millingen, Evelin 40, 43, 88, 90, 149, 150, 178
Polignac, palazzo 215
Poliziano 21, 48
Potter, Howard 149, 183
Primoli, Giuseppe 196
Prince, Morton 200, 201

Reynolds, Sir Joshua 53
Rezzonico, palazzo 84, 104, 138, 159, 186
Ricci, Sebastiano 22, 210, 211
Richetti 40, 194
Rietti 40
Rives, Amelia 190, 193
Rodd, Sir James Rennell 194, 195
Rogers family 104
Rombo family 191
Rombo Morosini, Annina 184, 185

Romney, George 172, 174
Rucellai, Cosimo 73
Ruskin, John 24, 28, 50, 58, 59, 63, 65, 71, 72, 73, 104
Russell, Henry 199, 201

Sagredo, palazzo 22
Sanderson, Sybil 194
Santomaso, Giuseppe 216
Sargent, John Singer 16, 24, 90, 156, 157, 159, 185, 186
Scamozzi, Vincenzo 21
Schuster, Frank 186
Semitecolo, palazzo 19, 31, 138, 139, 209
Shakespeare, William 38, 60
Shelley, Percy Bysshe 52
Shenstone, Ann 137, 139
Stein, Gertrude 166
Story, Julian Russell 201
Story, Waldo 155, 159, 181
Story, William Wetmore 52, 106, 159, 201
Sturges, Jonathan 152, 153
Symonds, John Addington 14, 132, 133, 184, 196

Taine, Hyppolite Adolphe 58, 71
Talleyrand, Charles-Maurice, Prince of 98
Tappan, Caroline Sturgis 137, 139
Tchiateff, Madame de 78, 79
Temple, Minnie 32
Tiepolo, Giambattista 22, 23, 36, 39, 49, 53, 211
Tilton, Paul 143
Tintoretto 28, 51, 58, 59, 60, 61, 63, 66
Tita 116, 120, 129
Titian 41, 53, 60, 66, 72, 104, 106, 172
Trevisan, palazzo 120

Van Dyck, Antonie 44, 53, 172
Venier dei Leoni, palazzo 19, 145

Vermeer, Jan 41
Veronese, Paolo 34, 52, 58, 60, 61, 69, 152
Victoria and Albert Museum 23
Viel, v. Wiel
Vitruvius 22
Vittoria, Alessandro 208, 211
Vulliany, Lewis 123

Wagner, Richard 46, 186
Wagnière Huntington, Laura, 91, 93, 117, 120, 197
Walsh, Catherine 25, 42, 95
Wharton, Edith 44, 53, 200, 201
Wiel, Alethea 117, 120

Wiel, Taddeo 122, 123
Wister, Sarah Butler 42, 85
Wolkoff, palazzo 19,186
Woolson, Constance Fenimore 29, 30, 31, 32, 51, 77, 83, 92
Wormeley Prescott, Katherine 88, 90, 95, 108, 119
Worth 40, 101, 102

Yriarte, Charles 194, 196

Zanchi, Antonio 210
Zorn, Anders 16, 24, 50
Zorzi, Alvise Piero 24, 50